For information about

DEPOSITIONS
PROCEDURES, STRATEGY AND TECHNIQUE
SECOND EDITION
(looseleaf edition)
by Paul M. Lisnek and Michael J. Kaufman

DEPOSITIONS: Procedures, Strategy and Technique, Professional Education Edition, designed for use in CLE settings, is the textual abridgement of a title in West's Litigation Library series. The section and form numbering of its looseleaf parent have been retained in the Professional Education Edition.

The abridgment process consisted of excising numerous whole sections and forms (as indicated in the Table of Contents); the fuller looseleaf also includes all forms on disk, so that they can be quickly displayed, edited, saved to your hard drive, or printed. Out of *DEPOSITIONS*, unabridged, you may create one general depositions notebook, or specific notebooks for individual cases. You may, by virtue of its looseleaf format, revise, add, or delete sections in developing your own approach to depositions practice.

For further information about, or to order the unabridged, looseleaf version of *DEPOSITIONS* with deposition forms on disc, please call West Publishing:

1–800–328–9352

WEST PUBLISHING COMPANY
610 Opperman Drive
P. O. Box 64526
St. Paul, MN 55164–0526

LITIGATION TOOLS
FROM WEST

LITIGATION LIBRARY

Depositions : Procedure, Strategy and Technique
(with Forms on Disk)
Lisnek and Kaufman

The Trialbook
(with Forms on Disk)
Sonsteng and Haydock

LAWYERING SKILLS SERIES

A Lawyer's Guide to Effective Negotiation and Mediation
Lisnek

Effective Client Communication:
A Lawyer's Handbook for Interviewing and Counseling
Lisnek

ADVOCACY:

Court Trials, Arbitrations, Administrative Cases, Jury Trials
Haydock and Sonsteng

The Common Sense Rules of Trial Advocacy
Evans

Bennett's Guide to Jury Selection and Trial Dynamics
Bennett and Hirschhorn

Federal Practice & Procedure
Wright, Miller, Kane, Cooper, Marcus, Graham and Gold

Manual For Complex Litigation

Reference Manual on Scientific Evidence

Courtroom Handbook on Federal Evidence
Goode and Wellborn

Federal Civil Rules Handbook
Baiker-McKee, Janssen, Berger and Corr

Handbook of Federal Evidence
Graham

LITIGATION TOOLS FROM WEST

Trial Advocacy
Jeans

Photographic Evidence
Scott

Federal Jury Practice and Instructions:
Civil and Criminal
Devitt, Blackmar, Wolff and O'Malley

Federal Court of Appeals Manual
Knibb

WESTLAW®
Specialized Litigation Databases

AFJ ....Almanac of the Federal Judiciary
AMJTA ....American Journal of Trial Advocacy
BNA-PLD.........................BNA Products Liability Daily
CA-JI ....California Jury Instructions
Expnet ....ExpertNet®
FSD.................................Forensic Services Directory
LITIG ....Litigation
LRP-JV ....Jury Verdicts and Settlement Summaries
LTG-TP............................Litigation Law Reviews, Texts and Journals
MEDMAL..........................Medical Malpractice Lawsuit Filings
REST-TORT ....Restatement of the Law: Torts
REVLITIG.........................The Review of Litigation
SCT-PREVIEW ....Preview of U.S. Supreme Court Cases
TASA...............................Technical Advisory Service for Attorneys
WTH-MDML.....................WESTLAW Topical Highlights-Medical Malpractice
WTH-PL ....WESTLAW Topical Highlights-Products Liability

WEST*fax*® West CD-ROM Libraries™ Disk Products

To order any of these trial practice tools, call your West
Representative or 1–800–328–9352.

NEED A NEW CASE RIGHT NOW?
You can get copies of new court cases faxed to
you today—at your office, courthouse or hotel, any-
where a fax machine is available. Call WEST*fax* at
1–800–562–2329.

March 1995

DEPOSITIONS:

PROCEDURE, STRATEGY AND TECHNIQUE

PROFESSIONAL EDUCATION EDITION

By

PAUL MICHAEL LISNEK, J.D., Ph.D.

President, Lisnek & Associates, Inc.
Vice President, National Institute for Legal Education

and

MICHAEL J. KAUFMAN, J.D.

Associate Professor of Law,
Loyola University of Chicago School of Law

ST. PAUL, MINN.
WEST PUBLISHING CO.
1995

 TEXT IS PRINTED ON 10% POST CONSUMER RECYCLED PAPER

 PRINTED WITH SOY INK™

DEDICATION

For my parents, Sandy and Seymour Lisnek, with
all my love—

P.M.L.

For my family—

M.J.K.

*

PREFACE

We live in a litigious society. The lawyer carries a burden to limit and focus pretrial efforts so that the ultimate resolution of a case, be it settlement or trial, is reached only after following full case evaluation and preparation. It would be grave error indeed to experience an adverse verdict as a result of inherently damaging admissions or otherwise impeachable testimony which could have been prevented through effective deposition preparation. Trial lawyers need to supervise the preparation and investigation of every case through the pretrial stage.

This book provides the planning mechanism for thorough preparation, execution and evaluation of depositions. The deposition provides the discovery mechanism for gathering and probing information by which the examiner measures the plausibility and potential success of his or her intended trial position.

Yet, the deposition is, in a sense, a radical departure from the adversary system. This discovery device often requires a party to provide the adversary with all of the evidence which that adversary needs to win the lawsuit. It compels one party to share with the adversary evidence helpful to that adversary. As such, the attorney who presents a client for deposition is often in a no-win situation. The best that the presenting attorney can hope to achieve in the deposition is damage control. That paramount goal of damage control is pursued in an interaction which is self-policing.

The new Federal Rules of Civil Procedure recognize the self-policing nature of the discovery and deposition process. They authorize mandatory prompt disclosure of relevant material prior to the deposition stage of discovery and establish presumptive limits on the number of depositions which each side may take in any litigation. Because those federal rules alter the procedural landscape in which depositions are taken, and because some states, such as Arizona, already have a comparable regime and other states are likely to follow, those federal rules are emphasized throughout this book. The appendices separately set forth the fundamental procedures governing depositions in those states with the greatest volume of litigation and in these states which have unique deposition practice. But, regardless of the rules which govern the deposition process, attorneys must develop effective techniques for taking and defending depositions. The primary goal of this book is to enable attorneys to understand the rules governing the deposition process, and to use those rules in a manner which produces successful and efficient depositions.

Supplementing the theoretical foundation from which the litigator prepares for deposition, this book provides a series of forms which enable the lawyer to apply directly the practical concepts to each case he or she is handling.

PREFACE

This book constitutes a step-by-step preparation guide assisting the attorney to decide which deposition to take or not take in each case. The attorney determines how each deposition can most effectively be taken, and how the information gathered from each deposition is to be integrated with the other pretrial mechanisms which comprise the discovery package. The outcome of any case is often hinged to the quality and depth of the depositions taken; it is well worth the attorney's time to both carefully read the concepts presented in this book and utilize those forms applicable in the attorney's own practice.

PAUL M. LISNEK
MICHAEL J. KAUFMAN

ACKNOWLEDGEMENTS

This second edition was prepared with the able assistance of several law students. The authors extend their sincere gratitude to the following students of Loyola University Chicago School of Law for their outstanding research: Lisa Madigan, Diane D'Onofrio, Gary Annes, William Atkins, William Bryant, Kim Egerman, Lisa Gruenberg, Margaret King, Christine Rogan and James Vlahakis.

Dr. Lisnek also extends appreciation to his assistants for their administrative support: Craig Balmer, Anne Brody and Richard Anton. As always, his warmest appreciation for the personal and professional support from Rick, Judy, David, Michael and Danielle Lisnek, David Jorbin, Arnold Pierson, Steve Pearson, Michael Mendelson, Cindy Raymond, Al Menotti, Bob Anderson, Julie Eichorn, Michael Menefee, Raymond Massey. Additional thanks to colleagues at the National Institute for Legal Education and Trial Logistics.

P.M.L.
M.J.K.

*

About the Authors

Paul M. Lisnek is formerly the assistant dean of Loyola University of Chicago School of Law where he taught negotiation, professional responsibility and pretrial litigation. He is currently the Vice President and Director of Mediator Training for Lawyers Mediation Service Corporation, the nation's only national network of law school deans, law professors, judges and seasoned litigators who work as mediators. He is also a senior trial consultant with Tsongas Associates, specializing in witness preparation and jury research and past president of the American Society of Trial Consultants. Dean Lisnek holds a law degree and Ph.D. in legal communication from the University of Illinois. He lectures across the country on lawyering and communication skills including negotiation, mediation, depositions, interviewing and counseling, and jury psychology. He is host of an award winning television talk show in Chicago, "Inside Your Government" and has served as a guest commentator on "Court TV." He is also director of academics of the National Law Program, and educational summer program for young adults interested in pursuing a career in law.

Michael J. Kaufman is a professor of law at Loyola University School of Law in Chicago and Of Counsel with Sachnoff & Weaver, Ltd. He has written several books and numerous law journal articles on topics litigation.

*

TABLE OF CONTENTS *

PART I. PREPARING FOR THE DEPOSITION

CHAPTER 1. THE TOOLS OF DISCOVERY

---

* Chapters and Sections in **boldface type** are found in this abridged edition intended for use in CLE programs. All other chapters can be found in the original edition only.

TABLE OF CONTENTS

CHAPTER 4. MATTERS TO CONSIDER BEFORE THE DEPOSITION

CHAPTER 5. VIDEOTAPED DEPOSITIONS

TABLE OF CONTENTS

CHAPTER 6. PRE–DEPOSITION PROCEDURES

PART II. THE DEPOSING ATTORNEY'S PERSPECTIVE

CHAPTER 7. EFFECTIVE DEPOSITION QUESTIONING

TABLE OF CONTENTS

TABLE OF CONTENTS

TABLE OF CONTENTS

TABLE OF CONTENTS

*

Part I

PREPARING FOR THE DEPOSITION

Chapter 1

THE TOOLS OF DISCOVERY

Table of Sections

§ 1.1 Introduction to the New Federal Rules of Civil Procedure

On December 1, 1993, proposed amendments to the Federal Rules of Civil Procedure became effective. The most significant change requires parties to meet to plan the discovery process and following the meeting, to disclose information relating to trial without formal request. Fed.R.Civ.P. 26(f). The primary purpose for the

DEPOSITIONS: Procedures, Strategy and Techniques, designed for use in CLE programs, is the textual abridgement of the looseleaf edition which includes forms on disk. The section and form numbering from the looseleaf edition have been retained in the Professional Education Edition.

change is to accelerate the exchange of information between the parties and to cut down on the paperwork required to request such information. Many district courts have successfully implemented similar requirements by local rule. Their experience shows that required disclosures save both parties time and money, especially when the parties first meet to discuss the issues in the case.

§ 1.5 Impact of Discovery Planning and Required Disclosures

The new rules encourage parties to plead with specificity and clarity. Broad, vague and conclusory allegations resulting from notice pleading will not impose an obligation on the responding party to search for and identify all persons involved in or documents pertaining to the allegation. However, clear and specific pleading will naturally lead to a more complete listing of relevant persons and documents.

It is a good idea for parties to have the discovery planning meeting early, even before the defendant answers or has time for more than a cursory investigation of the case, particularly when the claims in the complaint are broadly stated. Following an early meeting, parties can and should stipulate to a period of more than 10 days following the meeting to make disclosure one. For example, providing 10 days from the time the complaint is served is adequate and appropriate and will provide a period that is 2 weeks longer than the time formerly specified for responding to interrogatories served with the complaint.

The disclosure requirements do not preclude parties from using traditional discovery methods to gather additional information or to protect information from being discovered. For example, a party may ask an expert during a deposition about litigation testimony beyond the four-year period required by Rule 26(a)(2)(B). Likewise, the description of documents requirement in Rule 26(a)(1)(B) will not waive the disclosing party's right to

DEPOSITIONS: Procedures, Strategy and Techniques, designed for use in CLE programs, is the textual abridgement of the looseleaf edition which includes forms on disk. The section and form numbering from the looseleaf edition have been retained in the Professional Education Edition.

assert privilege or work product protection or to assert that the documents are not sufficiently relevant to justify the burden or expense of production.

Rule 26(a)(1) imposes the functional equivalent of a standing request for production under Rule 34. This obligation however, applies only to relevant documents not protected by privilege or work product. Likewise, a party is not expected to provide a damage calculation that depends on information possessed by another party or person (common in patent infringement cases). Parties have a continued obligation to disclose additional information as issues are developed and clarified. A party is not relieved from its obligation to disclose because another party has failed to disclose or has made an inadequate disclosure.

The expert report disclosure in Rule 26(a)(2)(B) should reduce the length of the expert's deposition or in some cases, the report may eliminate the need for a deposition entirely. The requirement for the report applies only to those experts who are retained or specially employed to testify. It does not apply, for example, to a treating physician. The report requirement can be waived by local rule, order, or written stipulation.

Disclosure three, pre-trial information, is made according to the schedules adopted by the court under Rule 16(b) or by special order. If the court does not adopt a schedule, disclosures must be made at least 30 days before commencement of the trial. Rule 26(a)(3)(A) requires, in part, a listing of all witnesses likely to be called to testify at trial. Rule 37(c)(1) provides that only persons so listed may testify at trial to present substantive evidence. However, an unlisted witness may be called to testify where his/her testimony is based upon developments during trial that could not reasonably have been anticipated. There is no obligation to secure the attendance of all persons listed, however, a party may be precluded from objecting if a person listed is called to testify by another party who did not list the person as a witness.

DEPOSITIONS: Procedures, Strategy and Techniques, designed for use in CLE programs, is the textual abridgement of the looseleaf edition which includes forms on disk. The section and form numbering from the looseleaf edition have been retained in the Professional Education Edition.

Notes

The exhibit and trial evidence disclosure in Rule 26(a)(3)(C) allows parties to describe categorically any items that are similar in nature. For example, unless the court has otherwise directed, a series of vouchers may be shown collectively as a single exhibit with their starting and ending dates. As with trial witnesses, unlisted exhibits and evidence may be used at trial if their need could not reasonably have been anticipated before trial.

Although the disclosure requirements seem rigid, they can be amended as long as both parties and the judge agree. Courts have the discretion to require more information than what is listed in the Rules or eliminate disclosure requirements entirely. Practically speaking, the disclosure requirements will vary from case to case depending on their complexity. The important thing is for all parties to keep an eye towards efficiency and cost savings. Proper discovery planning and disclosure obligations will help focus the discovery process and may facilitate settlement.

Form 35. Report of Parties' Planning Meeting

[Caption and Names of Parties]

1. Pursuant to Fed.R.Civ.P. 26(f), a meeting was held on ____(date)____ at ____(place)____ and was attended by:

____(name)____ for plaintiff(s)

____(name)____ for defendant(s) ____(party name)____

____(name)____ for defendant(s) ____(party name)____

2. Pre–Discovery Disclosures. The parties [have exchanged] [will exchange by ____(date)____] the information required by [Fed.R.Civ.P. 26(a)(1)] [local rule ——].

3. Discovery Plan. The parties jointly propose to the court the following discovery plan: [Use separate paragraphs or subparagraphs as necessary if parties disagree.]

DEPOSITIONS: Procedures, Strategy and Techniques, designed for use in CLE programs, is the textual abridgement of the looseleaf edition which includes forms on disk. The section and form numbering from the looseleaf edition have been retained in the Professional Education Edition.

Discovery will be needed on the following subjects:

<u>(brief description of subjects on which discovery will be needed)</u>

All discovery commenced in time to be completed by <u>(date)</u>. [Discovery on <u>(issue for early discovery)</u> to be completed by <u>(date)</u>.]

Maximum of __ interrogatories by each party to any other party. [Responses due __ days after service.]

Maximum of __ requests for admission by each party to any other party. [Responses due __ days after service.]

Maximum of __ depositions by plaintiff(s) and __ by defendant(s).

Each deposition [other than of _____] limited to maximum of __ hours unless extended by agreement of parties.

Reports from retained experts under Rule 26(a)(2) due:

from plaintiff(s) by <u>(date)</u>

from defendant(s) by <u>(date)</u>

Supplementations under Rule 26(e) due <u>(time(s) or interval(s))</u>.

4.   Other Items. [Use separate paragraphs or subparagraphs as necessary if parties disagree.]

The parties [request] [do not request] a conference with the court before entry of the scheduling order.

The parties request a pretrial conference in <u>(month and year)</u>.

Plaintiff(s) should be allowed until <u>(date)</u> to join additional parties and until <u>(date)</u> to amend the pleadings.

Defendant(s) should be allowed until <u>(date)</u> to join additional parties and until <u>(date)</u> to amend the pleadings.

All potentially dispositive motions should be filed by <u>(date)</u>.

DEPOSITIONS: Procedures, Strategy and Techniques, designed for use in CLE programs, is the textual abridgement of the looseleaf edition which includes forms on disk. The section and form numbering from the looseleaf edition have been retained in the Professional Education Edition.

Settlement [is likely] [is unlikely] [cannot be evaluated prior to ___(date)___] [may be enhanced by use of the following alternative dispute resolution procedure: [_____].

Final lists of witnesses and exhibits under Rule 26(a)(3) should be due from plaintiff(s) by ___(date)___ from defendant(s) by ___(date)___

Parties should have ___ days after service of final lists of witnesses and exhibits to list objections under Rule 26(a)(3).

The case should be ready for trial by ___(date)___ [and at this time is expected to take approximately ___(length of time)___].

[Other matters.]

Date: _____

COMMITTEE NOTES

This form illustrates the type of report the parties are expected to submit to the court under revised Rule 26(f) and may be useful as a checklist of items to be discussed at the meeting.

§ 1.6 Alternatives to Oral Deposition

Five traditional discovery methods exist as alternatives to an oral deposition:

(1) interrogatories;

(2) requests for the production of documents or other tangible material;

(3) physical or mental examinations;

(4) requests to admit; and

(5) written depositions. *See e.g.* Fed.R.Civ.P. 30–36.

Attorneys may employ any or all of these devices in a single case. Moreover, attorneys may use these discovery methods in any sequence. Accordingly, in developing a discovery strategy, attorneys should consider the

DEPOSITIONS: Procedures, Strategy and Techniques, designed for use in CLE programs, is the textual abridgement of the looseleaf edition which includes forms on disk. The section and form numbering from the looseleaf edition have been retained in the Professional Education Edition.

6

advantages and disadvantages of each discovery device in light of their discovery objectives.

§ 1.7 Discovery Objectives

Discovery performs both a systemic and an adversarial function. Pre-trial discovery enables the system of adjudication to reduce the genuine issues of material fact which must be resolved at trial. Also, discovery helps the system to weed out claims that may have been well-pled, but which, after discovery, turn out to have no basis in fact. Finally, discovery may encourage the settlement of disputes.

For the adversary, discovery is used *inter alia,* to:

(1) gather evidence for proof at trial;

(2) preserve evidence not available at trial;

(3) produce admissions which can be used at trial or in settlement negotiations;

(4) uncover claims or defenses previously unconsidered;

(5) foster settlement negotiations generally;

(6) reveal the strengths and weaknesses of potential trial witnesses; and

(7) refine theories of the case.

With these goals in mind, the attorney should evaluate each of the discovery alternatives.

§ 1.16 Written Depositions—Advantages and Disadvantages

A party may take and record the testimony of any person by compelling the person to answer a series of written questions under oath. Fed.R.Civ.P. 31.

Advantages

1. Written depositions generally may be taken without leave of court. Fed.R.Civ.P. 31(a)(1).

DEPOSITIONS: Procedures, Strategy and Techniques, designed for use in CLE programs, is the textual abridgement of the looseleaf edition which includes forms on disk. The section and form numbering from the looseleaf edition have been retained in the Professional Education Edition.

2. Before the commencement of an action, written depositions may be taken of any person with leave of court to perpetuate testimony. Fed.R.Civ.P. 27.

3. Written depositions may be taken of parties and non-parties. Fed.R.Civ.P. 31(a)(1).

4. Written depositions may be taken of corporations, partnerships, associations or governmental agencies, in which case the organization must appoint a knowledgeable agent to respond to the questions. Fed.R.Civ.P. 31(a)(3).

5. Although immediate follow-up questions are impossible, the rules do permit a series of follow-up, cross and re-direct questions. Fed.R.Civ.P. 31(a)(4).

6. The written deposition of a party or its designated agent may be used at trial by an adverse party for "any purpose." Fed.R.Civ.P. 32(a)(2).

7. The written deposition of a non-party may be used at trial for impeachment. Fed.R.Civ.P. 32(a)(1).

8. The written deposition of a non-party may be used at trial for any purpose if the non-party is unavailable. Fed.R.Civ.P. 32(a)(3).

9. The written deposition requires careful drafting, but is relatively inexpensive.

Disadvantages

1. Written depositions do not test the demeanor of the witness.

2. Responses to written depositions cannot immediately be followed-up.

3. Written depositions do not allow the deposing attorney to clarify questions.

§ 1.17 Use of Written Depositions

Written depositions have six valuable uses. First, unlike interrogatories, written depositions can be taken of non-parties. Accordingly, they provide the functional equivalent of interrogatories for non-parties. Second,

DEPOSITIONS: Procedures, Strategy and Techniques, designed for use in CLE programs, is the textual abridgement of the looseleaf edition which includes forms on disk. The section and form numbering from the looseleaf edition have been retained in the Professional Education Edition.

written depositions may be accompanied by a subpoena for documents under Fed.R.Civ.P. 45, in which case such documents can be discovered from a non-party. Third, written depositions provide a cost-effective alternative to oral depositions, particularly in smaller cases where the amounts in controversy may not warrant an expensive oral deposition of every witness. Fourth, written depositions allow the discovery of essential information from otherwise minor witnesses. Fifth, written depositions are useful to preserve the testimony of a witness who will not be available at trial. Finally, written depositions can be used to record the testimony of a friendly witness. Such a deposition is not only helpful at trial, but it may provide the basis for evidence supporting or opposing a summary judgment motion. Form 1–9 provides a method of cataloging the evidence received at a written deposition.

§ 1.18 Sequencing Discovery Devices—The Authority to Sequence

In litigation governed by a mandatory initial disclosure rule or court order, the parties will be unable to conduct any traditional discovery until after they have first met, conferred and exchanged information. *See, e.g.,* Fed.R.Civ.P. 26(d). After that mandatory disclosure conference, however, the "methods of discovery may be used in any sequence" unless the court orders, or the parties agree otherwise, Fed.R.Civ.P. 26(d). The discovery rules further allow the multiple use of each device. As a general rule, attorneys may freely craft a discovery plan or strategy which employs each of the devices in the most effective order.

Some limitations on this discovery freedom, however, should be kept in mind. First, discovery may not be taken *before* an action is commenced, except with leave of court to take a deposition to perpetuate testimony. Fed.R.Civ.P. 27. Second, in a lawsuit governed by a mandatory initial disclosure process, that process must be completed before additional discovery can be initiated.

DEPOSITIONS: Procedures, Strategy and Techniques, designed for use in CLE programs, is the textual abridgement of the looseleaf edition which includes forms on disk. The section and form numbering from the looseleaf edition have been retained in the Professional Education Edition.

Fed.R.Civ.P. 26(d). Third, the court has discretion to shorten or enlarge the time for responding to interrogatories, requests to produce or requests to admit, and can exercise that discretion so as to allow defendants enough time to secure counsel before responding to discovery requests. *See* Fed.R.Civ.P. 33, 34, 36. Fourth, the court and the parties must establish a plan and schedule of discovery which includes a discovery cut-off date. Fed.R.Civ.P. 26(f). Fifth, the court has authority pursuant to Fed.R.Civ.P. 26(c) to enter a protective order requiring that discovery be accomplished only at a certain time or by a certain method. Sixth, the district court has a duty in some cases to sequence discovery in a manner that will limit any burden on the responding party. *See, e.g.,* Marrese v. American Academy of Orthopaedic Surgeons, 726 F.2d 1150 (7th Cir.1984). Finally, in ordering a physical or mental examination, the court will consider whether alternative methods of discovering the same information can be explored, thus obviating the need for the exam. *See* Fed.R.Civ.P. 35.

§ 1.19 Developing a Sequence—The Pyramid Approach

The most common method of sequencing discovery is the pyramid approach. Under this approach, each discovery device builds on previous more general requests so that the information sought and obtained becomes increasingly detailed and precise. Attorneys aim their discovery requests at specific information, the importance of which has been made clear by prior requests or prior mandatory disclosures. The pyramid method also avoids unnecessary or duplicative discovery requests.

The following sequence is suggested by the pyramid method:

1. Mandatory Initial Disclosure of Relevant Information.

2. Interrogatories of a general nature served contemporaneously with the complaint or answer.

DEPOSITIONS: Procedures, Strategy and Techniques, designed for use in CLE programs, is the textual abridgement of the looseleaf edition which includes forms on disk. The section and form numbering from the looseleaf edition have been retained in the Professional Education Edition.

3. Requests for the production of documents served contemporaneously with the complaint or answer.

4. Depositions of parties and key witnesses.

5. Depositions of expert witnesses.

6. Physical or mental examinations, if any.

7. Requests to admit.

This scheme is designed primarily to discover facts. It exploits the fact-finding strengths of each of the discovery devices. Interrogatories are served to identify the status, personnel structure and other necessary background information about the adversary, the existence of documents and the identities of lay and expert witnesses. Once this information is disclosed, the discovering party can formulate requests to produce which seek information that actually exists. Further, the disclosure of the adversary's nature and status allows the discovering party to join additional parties. The revelation of key lay and expert witnesses also allows the discovering party to select productive deposition targets.

Under the pyramid approach, depositions are not taken until the deposing party has enough prior information from documents about the deponent to formulate the "right" questions. Finally, the effective deposition of an expert even about a narrow or complex area of the case often requires tremendous background material and preparation. As such, expert depositions are not taken until alternative discovery has been exhausted.

§ 1.20 Developing a Sequence—The Contention Approach

While the pyramid approach to discovery serves the goal of fact-finding or case-building, the "contention" approach to discovery serves the goal of dispute-elimination. The contention approach views discovery as a method of eliminating or reducing the genuine issues of fact between adversaries. Discovery is sequenced in a manner that fosters implicit or explicit admissions.

DEPOSITIONS: Procedures, Strategy and Techniques, designed for use in CLE programs, is the textual abridgement of the looseleaf edition which includes forms on disk. The section and form numbering from the looseleaf edition have been retained in the Professional Education Edition.

Further, because the ultimate goal of contention discovery is to eliminate the entire dispute among adversaries, the order of discovery should also account for litigation or settlement posturing.

Contention discovery thus may be used as follows:

1. Mandatory Initial Disclosure used in conjunction with "particularized" pleadings to insure prompt disclosure of key information and evidence.

2. A set of interrogatories served immediately after any mandatory disclosure conference that includes, (a) contention interrogatories seeking all of the evidence which supports each of the contentions in the adversary's pleadings, and (b) interrogatories seeking the identity of lay and expert witnesses.

3. A notice of deposition for the adversary served as soon as possible.

4. Requests to admit served as soon as possible which force the adversary to concede issues at an early stage of the litigation.

5. Notices of deposition immediately served upon each key witness as soon as their identities are known.

This rapid and difficult discovery pace forces the adversary to reveal its case, concede various issues, and makes settlement more attractive. Within this strategic order, the deposition is vital to obtaining admissions which can induce the rapid settlement of the litigation. The strategy is particularly effective when the discovering party moves for summary judgment at a relatively early stage. Under the Supreme Court's summary judgment standard, it is the party responding to the summary judgment motion who must obtain "specific facts showing that there is a genuine issue for a trial." See Celotex Corp. v. Catrett, 477 U.S. 317, 106 S.Ct. 2548, 91 L.Ed.2d 265 (1986); Fed.R.Civ.P. 56(c). Accordingly, the non-moving party assumes the burden of taking and

---

responding to discovery. Moreover, in responding to the summary judgment motion the nonmoving party must reveal to the moving party most, if not all, of the evidence which supports its theory of the case. Hence, even if the motion is denied, it has the strategic benefit of forcing the non-moving party to disclose its case.

§ 1.21   The Place of Depositions in the Sequence

The decision to depose and the timing of the deposition relative to alternative discovery devices hinges upon the attorney's discovery goals. Where the goal is fact-finding or case-building, the deposition should not be taken until after an adequate informational foundation has been established. Where the goal is dispute reduction, the deposition should be taken of the adversary and its key witnesses as soon as practicable. Form 1–12 provides a discovery sequence chart which can be used in evaluating the proper place of the deposition within the overall discovery plan.

§ 1.22   The Discovery Plan

The definition of discovery goals, the analysis of the effectiveness of each discovery device and the calculation of a proper sequence allow the attorney to develop a successful discovery plan. The ultimate goal of the discovery plan is a resolution of a dispute on terms favorable to the client. Where federal or state rules require the parties to meet at the inception of litigation to develop a discovery plan, the attorneys for each party must define their discovery goals before or during the pleading stage of litigation. The attorneys, however, should be prepared to modify their discovery plan as the litigation progresses. This modification requires negotiation and compromise throughout the litigation. Forms 1–13 and 1–14 enable the attorney to keep track of the "fruits" of discovery. They catalogue the information received in light of its value in building the attorney's own case or in destroying the adversary's case. The charts also make lucid the points of authorities which

---

DEPOSITIONS: Procedures, Strategy and Techniques, designed for use in CLE programs, is the textual abridgement of the looseleaf edition which includes forms on disk. The section and form numbering from the looseleaf edition have been retained in the Professional Education Edition.

still require some evidentiary support. Accordingly, the charts allow attorneys to take stock in the middle of litigation to determine whether additional discovery, perhaps in the form of depositions, is needed. They also permit attorneys to determine whether to seek a modification of any discovery plan which has been previously ordered or agreed to.

DEPOSITIONS: Procedures, Strategy and Techniques, designed for use in CLE programs, is the textual abridgement of the looseleaf edition which includes forms on disk. The section and form numbering from the looseleaf edition have been retained in the Professional Education Edition.

Form 1-9

Written Deposition Catalogue

Case _____   Account # _____

Witness	Notice Served & Subpoena Served	Response	Deposition Date/Time	Transcript Received	Deposition Signed	Deposition Filed

Form 1-9

[G20,481]

15

Form 1-10

Oral Deposition Catalogue

Case _____ Account # _____

Witness	Notice Served & Subpoena Served	Response	Deposition Date/Time	Transcript Received	Deposition Signed	Deposition Filed

Form 1-10

[G20,482]

Form 1-11

Discovery Alternatives Chart

Method	Definition	Party or NonParty	Limitations	Timing	Response	Method of Service
Interrogatories	Series of written questions served by a party which must be answered fully and separately, in writing and under oath. Fed.R.Civ. P. 33(a).	Party only; but may use written depositions for non-parties. Fed.R.Civ. P. 33(a); 31.	25 including all discreet Subparts. Fed.R.Civ. P. 33(a).	Anytime after parties meet to plan discovery, absent leave of court or written stipulation. Fed.R.Civ. P. 33(a); 26(d).	30 Days; a shorter or longer time may be directed by the court or agreed to in writing by the parties. Fed.R.Civ. P. 33(b)(3); 29.	Mail
Requests for Production	A party may serve upon another party a request to produce, or to enter land to inspect, documents or tangible thing in the possession, custody or control of the other party. Fed.R.Civ. P. 34(a).	Party only; but may accompany notice of deposition of a non-party with a Rule 45 subpoena for documents. Fed.R.Civ. P. 45.	None	Anytime after parties meet to plan discovery, absent leave of court or written stipulation. Fed.R.Civ. P. 34(b); 26(d).	30 days; a shorter or longer time may be directed by court or agreed to in writing by the parties. Fed.R.Civ. P. 34(b); 29	Mail
Physical and Mental Examinations	A party may move to compel another party to undergo a mental or physical examination. Fed.R.Civ. P. 35(a).	Party or its agents only. Fed.R.Civ. P. 35(a).	None	Anytime, with leave. Fed.R.Civ. P. 35(a).	Specified in court order. Fed.R.Civ. P. 35(a).	Court order; detailed written report of findings must be delivered. Fed.R.Civ. P. 35(b).
Requests to Admit	A party may serve on another party a request that the other party admit opinions, facts, the application of law to fact or the genuineness of documents. Fed.R.Civ. P. 36.	Party only. Fed.R.Civ. P. 36.	None	Anytime after parties meet to plan discovery, absent leave of court or written stipulation. Fed.R.Civ. P. 36(a); 26(d).	30 days; or as the parties may agree to in writing. Admitted if not denied. Fed.R.Civ. P. 36(a); 29.	Mail
Written Deposition	A party may take and record the testimony of any person by compelling the person to answer a series of written questions under oath. Fed.R.Civ. P. 31.	Written deposition may be taken of both parties and non-parties. Fed.R.Civ. P. 31(a).	10 -- including those taken under Rule 30 unless otherwise provided by leave of court of written Stipulation. Fed.R.Civ. P. 31(a).	Before commencement of the action with leave of court to perpetuate testimony Fed.R.Civ. P. 27. After commencement of the action, they may be taken after parties meet to plan discovery, absent leave of court or written stipulation. Fed.R.Civ. P. 31(c); 26(d).	At a reasonable and convenient time, typically by agreement.	
Oral Deposition	A Party may take and record the testimony of any person upon oral examination. Fed.R.Civ. P. 30.	Oral deposition may be taken of both parties and non-parties. Fed.R.Civ. P. 30(a).	10 -- including those taken under Rule 51 unless otherwise provided by leave of court or written stipulation. Fed.R.Civ. P. 30(a).	Before commencement of the action, with leave of court to perpetuate testimony. Fed.R.Civ. P. 27. After commencement of the action only after parties meet to plan discovery, absent leave of court or written stipulation. Fed.R.Civ. P. 31, 26(d).	At a reasonable and convenient time, typically by agreement.	

Form 1-11

[G20,483]

17

Method	Leave of Court Required	Control of Response or Follow-up	Expense	Efficacy	Use at Trial	Notes
Interrogatories	yes, if a party plans to serve interrogatories before the parties meet to plan discovery. Fed.R.Civ. P. 33(a).	none	minimal	-- general background information, -- identity of lay and expert witness; -- status of other parties -- contention interrogatories	-- Evidentiary Admissions; impeachment.	
Requests for Production	yes, if a party plans to serve requests for production before the parties meet to plan discovery. Fed.R.Civ. P. 34(b).	none	moderate particularly in organization and review of documents.	-- discovery of candid information from an adversary prepared before litigation. -- discovery of business records which can be admitted at trial.	-- Exhibits admissible under business record exception to the hearsay cite rule.	
Physical and Mental Examinations	yes; affirmative showing of good cause to take exam and that the material discovered is probative of an issue in controversy.	none	significant; examining physician is an expert who must be reimbursed.	-- produce unalterable evidence of physical or mental condition; -- have great settlement value -- may induce the elimination of issues in controversy.	-- Admissibility at trial as an expert's report.	
Requests to Admit	yes, if a party plans to serve requests to admit before the parties meet to plan discovery. Fed.R.Civ. P. 36(a).	none; but self-executing sanction for failure to respond.	minimal	-- eliminate matters not in dispute -- obtain admissions for use at trial -- obtain admissions for use in summary judgment.	-- Conclusive admissions at trial.	
Written Deposition	no, unless sought before commencement of action to perpetuate testimony, Fed.R.Civ. P. 27, 31, or sought as to an expert witness, Fed.R.Civ. P. 26, or sought before the parties meet to plan discovery. Fed.R.Civ. P. 31, 26(d).	little; may serve follow-up questions. Fed.R.Civ. P. 31(a).	minimal	-- functional equivalent of interrogatories for non-parties -- functional equivalent of document request for non-parties when accompanied by Rule 45 subpoena -- cost effective alternative to oral depositions -- record of testimony of unavailable, minor or friendly witness.	-- Deposition of a party or unavailable non-party by adverse party for any purpose -- Deposition of an available non-party used mainly for impeachment.	
Oral Deposition	no, unless sought before commencement of action to perpetuate testimony, Fed.R.Civ. P. 27, 30, or sought as to an expert witness, Fed.R.Civ. P. 26, or sought before parties meet to plan discovery. Fed.R.Civ. P. 30, 26(d).	substantial	significant	-- parties and key witnesses -- discovery of detailed litigation-provoking facts -- party, rather than attorney, responds -- establish and lock-in adverse version of facts -- assess demeanor of witness -- insight into trial.	-- Deposition of a party of unavailable non-party used by an adverse party for any purpose. -- Deposition of an available non-party used mainly for impeachment.	

Form 1-11 (continued)
[G20,484]

18

Form 1-12

Discovery Sequence Chart

Method	Limit on Discovery Sequencing	Role in Fact-Building	Role in Dispute-Reduction	Notes
Interrogatories	1. Defendant has 30 days to respond. Fed.R.Civ. P. 33. 2. A shorter or longer time may be directed by the court or agreed to in writing by the parties. Fed.R.Civ. P. 33. 3. Court may order that contention interrogatories not be answered until "after designated discovery." Fed.R.Civ. P. 33(c). 4. Rule 26(c) protective order 5. Rule 26(d) sequencing 6. Request limited to 25, including all discreet subparts. Fed.R.Civ. P. 33(a).	1. Identities of lay and expert witness 2. Existence of documents 3. Reveal status and employment structure of adversary 4. Disclose related events or transaction	1. Contention interrogatories 2. Identities of lay and expert witnesses	
Requests to Produce	1. Defendant has 30 days to respond. Fed.R.Civ. P. 34. 2. A shorter or longer time may be directed by the court or agreed to in writing by the parties. Fed.R.Civ. P. 34. 3. Rule 26(c) protective order 4. Rule 26(d) sequencing	1. Pre-litigation records of parties 2. Background memoranda	1. Admissions in business records 2. Smoking guns 3. Disclosure of privileged information 4. Creates burdens, particularly for small business	
Physical and Mental Examinations	1. Alternative methods of discovery explored first. Fed.R.Civ. P. 35. 2. Rule 26(c) protective order 3. Rule 26(d) sequencing	1. Evidence of mental or physical condition of parties, where condition is in controversy	1. Induces admissions of matters previously in controversy 2. Induces settlement	

Form 1-12
[G20,485]

19

Method	Limit on Discovery Sequencing	Role in Fact-Building	Role in Dispute-Reduction	Notes
Requests to Admit	1. Defendant has 30 days to respond. Fed.R.Civ. P. 36 2. Court may shorten or enlarge time for response or parties may agree to do so in writing. Fed.R.Civ. P. 36 3. Although Rule 36 limits the availability of the "lack of information" response to a request to admit, that response if more plausible at an early age stage of litigation. 4. Rule 26(c) protective order 5. Rule 26(d) sequencing	1. Genuineness of documents 2. Fact Admissions	1. Eliminates issues in dispute 2. Sets up summary judgment	
Written Depositions	1. Notice; custom of reasonableness 2. Rule 26(c) protective order 3. Rule 26(d) sequencing 4. Limited to 10, including those taken under Rule 30, unless otherwise provided by court or written stipulation. Fed.R.Civ. P. 31(a).	1. To perpetuate testimony if before action. 2. Interrogatories for non-parties 3. Document request for non-parties 4. Record of testimony for unavailable, minor or unfriendly witnesses.	1. Admissions 2. Locking testimony 3. Impeachment	
Oral Depositions	1. Notice; custom of reasonableness and convenience. 2. Limited to 10, including those taken under Rule 31, unless otherwise provided by court or written stipulation. Fed.R.Civ. P. 30(a).	1. Discovery of detailed litigation provoking facts 2. Discovery of information from parties and key witnesses	1. Testimony from party rather than attorney 2. Establish and lock-in adversary's version of facts 3. Assess witness demeanor 4. Intimidation 5. Insight into trial behavior 6. Impeachment 7. Admissions 8. Use at trial against adversary for any purpose	

Form 1-12 (continued)

[G20,486]

20

Chapter 2

PLANNING TO TAKE DEPOSITIONS

Table of Sections

---

§ 2.1 Deciding to Take the Deposition—The Factors

The decision to take a deposition requires evaluation of each potential deponent's knowledge of the case and his importance to the litigation; such decision is reached within the framework of purposes served by taking the deposition. While alternative discovery tools may uncover particular information, Form 2–1 permits attorneys to evaluate with ease the need for a deposition by reviewing all relevant considerations in a summary chart format.

Form 2–1 requires the attorney to specify the role each prospective deponent serves in the case vis-a-vis the

---

DEPOSITIONS: Procedures, Strategy and Techniques, designed for use in CLE programs, is the textual abridgement of the looseleaf edition which includes forms on disk. The section and form numbering from the looseleaf edition have been retained in the Professional Education Edition.

21

relevant case issues and what that witness has to say or can prove with regard to each such issue. Beyond these considerations, the attorney also states why this information is needed through an importance rating scale. By evaluating the *alternative* means of obtaining that same information, the attorney can best decide whether each deposition should or should not be taken in the case.

Once completing Form 2–1's summary chart, the attorney considers the summary of the case issues en toto along with the importance ratings and indicates whether the deposition is one which must, should, is desirable to, should not or must not be taken. A section for comments and reasoning permits the attorney to memorialize the decision should he wonder at a later date whether such deposition was or is indeed necessary.

While attorney opinion may change regarding whether a deposition should be taken, it is important that the lawyers monitor their pretrial decisions through the litigation. Form 2–2 tracks the depositions taken as discovery proceeds, by providing a record of each party deposed, the name of the presenting attorney and relevant deposition information, including the court reporter service used and whether or not the transcript was ordered. A follow-up section requires the attorney to indicate the completion of transcript review, signature and filing. The latter part of the form monitors non-party witness addresses by requiring updating on a regular basis, thereby preventing loss of contact with non-party witnesses.

It is too often the case that a witness is unable to be located at the time of deposition or trial. As non-parties to the litigation, these witnesses cannot be expected to possess loyalty to the attorneys or the legal process; they may very well move their domicile without notifying anyone related to the litigation. If the non-party witness is not a close friend of or otherwise related to a party, it is unlikely that this person will be easily found. Indicating the source of the address information means a

DEPOSITIONS: Procedures, Strategy and Techniques, designed for use in CLE programs, is the textual abridgement of the looseleaf edition which includes forms on disk. The section and form numbering from the looseleaf edition have been retained in the Professional Education Edition.

detective or other tracing service can better track down the witness should contact be lost.

§ 2.2 Advantages of Taking an Oral Deposition

Oftentimes, lawyers view depositions as an expensive discovery tool for which a better substitute should often be found. Nevertheless, several purposes are served by taking a deposition:

(1) An oral deposition may be taken without leave of court after any mandatory initial disclosure conference. Fed.R.Civ.P. 30(a)(2)(c).

(2) Before the commencement of an action, an oral deposition may be taken of any person with leave of court to perpetuate testimony. Fed. R.Civ.P. 27.

(3) An oral deposition may be taken of parties and non-parties. Fed.R.Civ.P. 30(a).

(4) An oral deposition may be taken of a corporation, partnership, association or governmental agency, in which case the organization must designate an agent to testify on its behalf. Fed.R.Civ.P. 30(b)(6).

(5) Oral depositions are taken under oath. Fed. R.Civ.P. 30(c).

(6) The testimony taken at an oral deposition is recorded. Fed.R.Civ.P. 30(b)(4).

(7) The oral deposition of a party or its designated agent may be used by an adverse party for "any purpose." Fed.R.Civ.P. 32(a)(2).

(8) The oral deposition may be taken by telephone or other remote electronic means such as satellite television. Fed.R.Civ.P. 30(b)(7).

(9) An oral deposition may be videotaped. Fed. R.Civ.P. 30(b)(2).

(10) Evidence taken at an oral deposition is generally received subject to objections. Fed.R.Civ.P. 30(c).

DEPOSITIONS: Procedures, Strategy and Techniques, designed for use in CLE programs, is the textual abridgement of the looseleaf edition which includes forms on disk. The section and form numbering from the looseleaf edition have been retained in the Professional Education Edition.

(11) A wide range of sanctions is available if the deponent fails to appear or cooperate in the deposition. Fed.R.Civ.P. 30(g); 37.

(12) Depositions enable an attorney to gather and probe information from opposing parties, witnesses, and anyone with knowledge directly or indirectly related to the case at bar.

(13) The information gathered and explored may be conducted over a period of a few hours, and not over the several weeks it might otherwise take to obtain answers to written interrogatories.

(14) The stagnant format of written interrogatory questions are no match for the spontaneous and flexible questioning or follow-up which deposition structure permits.

(15) Depositions enable the attorney to place limitations on and establish boundaries around the information disclosed by the deponent.

(16) The attorney can confirm the details of the deponent's story with previous statements made by or records of that deponent or other documents relating to that deponent's story.

(17) The adversary's story or position which runs contrary to your side can be identified through a deposition of either the adversary or a neutral deponent. These witnesses may possess damaging information which will highlight any weaknesses in the examining attorney's *own* case.

(18) The examiner can measure the demeanor for trial of potentially damaging witnesses.

(19) The appearance of one's *own* client and witnesses can be monitored.

(20) Testimony can be established to be used as admissions, for impeachment, or for other relevant evidentiary purposes at trial.

(21) Deposition preserves testimony of a witness not able to appear at trial because of age, illness, imprisonment, distance, death or other exceptional factors which prevent attendance.

DEPOSITIONS: Procedures, Strategy and Techniques, designed for use in CLE programs, is the textual abridgement of the looseleaf edition which includes forms on disk. The section and form numbering from the looseleaf edition have been retained in the Professional Education Edition.

Where testimony will be supportive or of value, the attorney may anticipate one of these problems and proceed with the deposition.

(22) Testimony of witnesses, such as certain tightly-scheduled medical experts, can be recorded.

(23) Depositions narrow and clarify issues for trial.

(24) The examiner establishes credibility both with the deponent and other attorneys present, all of whom will be conducting a similar evaluation of their own.

(25) Testimony can be established to encourage settlement of the litigation.

(26) A relationship can be established with the deponent depending on the goals of the examiner. For example, an attorney may wish to create comraderie or adversity with the deponent as a means of posturing for subsequent settlement demands.

§ 2.3 Disadvantages of Taking an Oral Deposition

(1) The party taking the deposition must give reasonable notice of the deposition to the deponent and to every other party to the action. Fed.R.Civ.P. 30(b)(1).

(2) Under the federal rules, each "side" in the litigation is limited to ten depositions, unless the court orders, or the parties agree in writing, otherwise. Fed.R.Civ.P. 30(a)(2)(A).

(3) Where the witness is a non-party, a subpoena ad testificandum must be served in accordance with Federal Rule 45. Witness and mileage fees must accompany the subpoena.

(4) The oral deposition of a non-party witness must generally take place within 100 miles of where the witness works, transacts business or resides. Fed.R.Civ.P. 45. Accordingly, attorneys must do the bulk of traveling to take a non-party's deposition.

DEPOSITIONS: Procedures, Strategy and Techniques, designed for use in CLE programs, is the textual abridgement of the looseleaf edition which includes forms on disk. The section and form numbering from the looseleaf edition have been retained in the Professional Education Edition.

(5) The deponent typically reserves the right to make changes in the deposition transcript before signing the transcript. Fed.R.Civ.P. 30(e).

(6) In practice, an oral deposition sometimes becomes an occasion for abusive tactics and attorney speechifying. The adversarial nature of the face-to-face confrontation and the absence of a neutral arbiter can combine to create an atmosphere of tension in which the attorneys "testify" more than do the clients.

(7) Some attorneys claim depositions are an expensive discovery tool. The expense of taking one, however, is more often outweighed by the considerable time and money spent both in executing written interrogatories and handling the numerous motions and hearings for compliance and sanctions held as a consequence.

(8) Depositions require a potentially unprepared adversary to review the file and to be ready for the deposition and, ultimately, trial. Assumed in this reasoning is the preparation of trial strategy and establishment of a settlement posture by the adversary. However, a deposition taken early in the litigation, prior to investigation and study by the opponent, may produce helpful admissions.

(9) Depositions potentially place the examining attorney's trial strategy on the table and can alert the adversary to the existence of witnesses, thereby educating not only the deponent but the adversarial attorney. Of course, written discovery may similarly, albeit subtly, educate the opponent on case theory thereby shaping subsequent testimony.

(10) A witness can only be deposed one time in any litigation without leave of court. Fed.R.Civ.P. 30(a)(2)(B).

The utility of the information obtained by the examiner will likely outweigh this often illusory disadvantage. The information received will be of greater value than

DEPOSITIONS: Procedures, Strategy and Techniques, designed for use in CLE programs, is the textual abridgement of the looseleaf edition which includes forms on disk. The section and form numbering from the looseleaf edition have been retained in the Professional Education Edition.

the educating disclosure; the deposition will have been worth the effort. In a skillfully conducted deposition, the adverse party receives few helpful disclosures beyond a general awareness of the complexity of the litigation.

(11) Witnesses are rehearsed for trial through deposition, highlighting areas for improvement in both presentation and content of trial testimony. Much of the confidence gained is illusory since deposition testimony is taken in an attorney's office, outside the tension inherent in the courtroom environ.

(12) Depositions establish and preserve the testimony of the deponent which may necessitate modification in case strategy and presentation. Effective question design by the examiner, in which only information needed to pin down certain testimony is sought, can minimize the risk.

(13) Informal discovery may be an effective means for uncovering facts, but does not substitute for the deposition. While an attorney can speak with any non-party witness without notifying the opposing lawyer, it is improper to speak with an opposing party without the consent of his/her attorney (ABA Model Code of Professional Responsibility DR 7–104). Moreover, a non-party witness may deny at trial having made any previous statement.

(14) A deposition preserves testimony harmful to the lawyer's case which might otherwise have been unavailable at the time of trial. It is therefore advisable to evaluate and consider postponing the deposition of a witness expected to give harmful testimony.

After considering all of the disadvantages, there should be little doubt that deposition is the best tool available for pretrial discovery purposes. It permits the examining attorney to gather and probe information first-hand while simultaneously establishing the credibility of the

DEPOSITIONS: Procedures, Strategy and Techniques, designed for use in CLE programs, is the textual abridgement of the looseleaf edition which includes forms on disk. The section and form numbering from the looseleaf edition have been retained in the Professional Education Edition.

deponent who will likely testify at trial. Such information is invaluable to effective trial preparation.

§ 2.4 Scope of Depositions

Federal and state rules of procedure permit broad discovery including deposition questions, which are designed to lead to the production of admissible evidence. The questions need not produce answers which are themselves admissible at trial. *See, e.g.,* Fed.R.Civ.P. 26(b). Accordingly, deposition questions may seek any information which is arguably relevant to the subject matter of the claims or defenses in the litigation. *Id.*

Determining the probative value and relevance of particular questions asked in depositions is often a difficult task, however, since there is great variance in custom and practice among locations. In reality, most problems which arise during depositions are resolved through cooperative attitudes and relationships between the attorneys. While there is no specific scope which defines deposition questions, there are boundaries beyond which attorneys will not permit a question to be posed. No judge is present to resolve disagreements, so the attorneys must exercise goodwill, guided by custom and practice, but modified by both their strategic motivation, and the nature of the relationship between the attorneys present. Maintaining good relations with fellow litigators, though they are often adversaries by definition, is more often recommended than not to produce peaceful resolution to disputes.

Fed.R.Civ.P. 29 specifically permits attorneys to take depositions in any mutually agreed upon manner; problems which cannot be resolved by the attorneys may be resolved through the judicial mechanism provided by Fed.R.Civ.P. 37. No substantial body of case law exists which would permit a directive resolution of many issues; judges necessarily turn to the governing practice and custom of the locale.

The rules governing deposition procedures extend to the determination of where the deposition will be held

(Fed.R.Civ.P. 30(b)(1)). While plaintiffs and their agents are required to be available in the district where the action is pending, depositions of corporate officers or employees will usually be taken at the principal place of business. Special circumstances including hardship or financial burden on a particular party are factors which may lead a court to change the location of a deposition.

While the exact location of a deposition is often dependent upon attorney choice, the deposition is most commonly taken in the examining attorney's office. The deposition of a non-party witness, such as a medical expert, is often taken at that person's office; this strategy establishes good relations with the non-party witness, thus not antagonizing the witness.

Selecting the location of a deposition necessarily reflects the relationship intended to be established between the deponent and the examiner. While taking the deposition of a party at the party's attorney's office would provide the deponent with a familiar and comfortable surrounding, such an environ may or may not be desirable for the examiner, who usually notices the deposition at his/her own examiner's office. The examiner's office provides better control over the interaction and over interruptions.

§ 2.5 The Need for the Story

What is this case all about? Seemingly a simple question, it rarely gets asked. Rather, the associate is asked to "cover the deposition" by finding out what the deponent knows. It seems to matter little what is known about the case, its history, or its vulnerable parts. In reality, these things matter greatly and need to be uncovered prior to taking any deposition.

The fundamental premise to keep in mind prior to taking any deposition is that there is little reality in the case. Clients and witnesses report what they remember and what they report is tainted by their biased tainted memories. It is natural to forget details over time, add details that support one's position and become commit-

DEPOSITIONS: Procedures, Strategy and Techniques, designed for use in CLE programs, is the textual abridgement of the looseleaf edition which includes forms on disk. The section and form numbering from the looseleaf edition have been retained in the Professional Education Edition.

ted to explanations that serve to exonerate, regardless of whether they can be objectively supported. Therefore, it is important to evaluate the strength of the case shortly after the client is interviewed, or the file is opened. Of course, it is essential to conduct a thorough and effective initial interview of the client. (See Paul M. Lisnek, *Effective Client Communication: A Lawyer's Guide to Interviewing and Counseling,* West Publishing Company, St. Paul, Minnesota, 1992).

Once the initial information is gathered, the responsible lawyer should create an understanding of the case story or account as it could be told at trial. Then, during a lawyers' luncheon, or some other firm-based meeting, the responsible lawyer should report the intake of the case to the other lawyers by telling the client's story. The others who listen to the account are in a strong position to evaluate and analyze the case, identifying the weaknesses, holes and inconsistencies. Discovery and depositions become the tools for testing, modifying and solidifying the ultimate account that will be told to a judge or jury should the case reach trial. The model for this system is the storytelling model developed for use at trial (see W. Lance Bennett and Martha S. Feldman, *Reconstructing Reality in the Courtroom: Justice and Judgment in American Culture,* Rutgers University Press, 1981).

§ 2.6 Developing the Story Through Deposition

Listening to the client's account in the form of a story enables the lawyer to determine whether the opposing counsel, the judge or jury could view the story as internally consistent, coherent and more complete than the adversary's competing story. Unless a settlement is reached, the parties' competing renditions of the underlying events related in trial will be weighed by either judge or jury as the means for determining a verdict. Paul M. Lisnek, *Effective Client Communication: A Lawyer's Guide to Interviewing and Counseling,* West Publishing Company, St. Paul, Minnesota, 1992; sec. 5.3.

DEPOSITIONS: Procedures, Strategy and Techniques, designed for use in CLE programs, is the textual abridgement of the looseleaf edition which includes forms on disk. The section and form numbering from the looseleaf edition have been retained in the Professional Education Edition.

The adversary process, by definition, produces two conflicting accounts of the same set of events. The decision maker will weigh the competing testimony, uncover discrepancies and determine the more plausible explanation for the events in question.

The storytelling model can be used to both create and understand the account of events a client seeks to relate. Storytelling permits both lawyer and client to communicate effectively through the vast amount of information which must be related to and processed by the jury. W. Lance Bennett, *Storytelling in Criminal Trials: A Model of Social Judgment,* 64 Quarterly Journal of Speech (1978) at 1–22). The model provides a framework for understanding how juries process information. As such, the model presents a basis for attorneys to use in preparing for and taking depositions. In addition, the information related by a lawyer's own client and witnesses in their depositions is equally important to the stability and development of the case account or story.

"Storytelling" as the method for gathering information makes perfect sense. The events which underlie the client's problem are in the past; they will be relived only through the client's recitation. By definition, every event is a thing of the past; there is no objective reality to be related. Past events cannot be accurately recreated. The only reality that will ever exist is the re-telling of past events as they occurred from the client's perspective. Past events are not re-created, they are created and shaped by the client's subjective view of reality grounded in experience. The only reality of past events that can ever be created is subjective and the result of the client's selective memories. Paul M. Lisnek, *Effective Client Communication: A Lawyer's Guide to Interviewing and Counseling,* West Publishing Company, St. Paul, Minnesota, 1992; sec. 5.3.

The selective creation of past events ultimately produces three versions in every case: the plaintiff's, the defendant's and the truth. The latter likely lies some-

DEPOSITIONS: Procedures, Strategy and Techniques, designed for use in CLE programs, is the textual abridgement of the looseleaf edition which includes forms on disk. The section and form numbering from the looseleaf edition have been retained in the Professional Education Edition.

where in between the subjective and tainted perspectives of both parties. Depositions, among other discovery tools, permit the lawyer to test these perspectives both substantively, and in terms of the credibility of the deponent. The search for reality includes the extent to which the deponent is committed to his or her account and the degree to which a judge or jury can be expected to believe that account.

§ 2.7 Using the Storytelling Model

The story becomes the organizer of information which enables the lawyer in deposition to perform two interpretive operations: first, locate the key or central action in the case—*i.e.,* the event that needs to be explained, or is in dispute. Second, the lawyer constructs the most credible inferences between the elements of information related by the client which create consistency, completeness and coherence in the story. The story becomes the test against which the adversary's competing account will be compared by a jury. Paul M. Lisnek, *Jury Selection Process: A Psychological Perspective,* 4 CBA Record 1 (January, 1990), at 27.

The story must be internally consistent. Even the weakest points of the case must be fit into the story to measure the extent to which a finder of fact could find the story to be realistic. A scale from maximum to least believability can be pictured as the lawyer attempts to envision how a judge or jury would likely see the client's story compared to that of the opponent. The lawyer needs to determine whether the various inferences that create the story are realistic, viable and compatible in light of what is known about similar occurrences and their own experiences in the real world. Paul M. Lisnek, *Effective Client Communication: A Lawyer's Guide to Interviewing and Counseling,* West Publishing Company, St. Paul, Minnesota, 1992; sec. 5.4.

A lawyer evaluates the cast of characters involved in the story and envisions how a finder of fact will view the motivation of each party. This is part of what depositions are all about. Note the planning required and the grave error made when one assumes that the deposition is merely about finding out what the deponent knows. The lawyer wants to uncover how each deponent's personal agenda can influence the strength of the case. A story determined to be inconsistent, incomplete or incoherent sends a message to the lawyers that they may not be getting the whole story. *Id.*

At each stage of the story creating process, the lawyer decides how many different interpretations can be given to each story element, what possible alternative connections can be established between the elements, and what general frame of reference or perspective a jury could apply. This is what needs to be tested in each deposition; this is what needs to be protected in the deposition of one's own client.

In effect, lawyers, like jurors, ask themselves whether an event *could* have happened in the way related by the client, and whether it *did* happen in the manner suggested by the story. Certainly at trial, the side which creates the more credible story will likely achieve the favorable verdict. The lawyer thinks ahead to these evaluations and must test them through each of the depositions taken in the case.

Form 2–3 presents the storytelling model in a form which permits the lawyer to apply it directly to any case. The form is to be used in the initial client interview and modified as the case continues and develops. The bits of evidence are recorded under the appropriate party (plaintiff or defendant); the connecting inferences are marked which bind the elements together. The areas of the story which are inconsistent, incoherent or incomplete should become evident. The lawyer should identify those areas which must be clarified or probed further through depositions and discovery. *Id.* Lawyers keep abreast of the internal strength of their own client's story.

DEPOSITIONS: Procedures, Strategy and Techniques, designed for use in CLE programs, is the textual abridgement of the looseleaf edition which includes forms on disk. The section and form numbering from the looseleaf edition have been retained in the Professional Education Edition.

Form 2–4 assesses the adversary's story by evaluating the information gathered in Form 2–3. As lawyers consider what information will be offered by the other side, they must also give thought to the counter response they can create through depositions. Thus, the lawyer not only works with the client to insure a strongly presented story, but can uncover the inconsistencies or gaps in the adversary's story as well.

The following examples illustrate how the model works in practice. In a civil case:

1) Central Common Element: Plaintiff is injured while using an electric hedge trimmer in his backyard. This fact is common to both parties' stories and is agreed to by both parties. The dispute between parties arises in how and why the occurrence happened.

2) Plaintiff's story (presented in separate testimony by witnesses whose stories combine to create the whole):

   a) The equipment was improperly designed (expert)

   b) The equipment was improperly manufactured (expert)

   c) The equipment lacked proper safety features (expert)

   d) The plaintiff's conduct was proper and now he suffers great and ongoing pain and injury (plaintiff)

   e) Plaintiff's life is disrupted (spouse)

   f) Plaintiff has undergone and will continue to undergo medical procedures and medication (medical testimony)

Additional pieces of testimony are added to the whole picture. Each must continue to fit together with the testimony that precedes it.

DEPOSITIONS: Procedures, Strategy and Techniques, designed for use in CLE programs, is the textual abridgement of the looseleaf edition which includes forms on disk. The section and form numbering from the looseleaf edition have been retained in the Professional Education Edition.

The defense will provide testimony that contradicts the expert testimony regarding design and manufacture. The key testimony will need to dispute the factual elements of the case. For example, the defense will attempt to illustrate on cross examination that the plaintiff did not exercise due care and proper conduct. The defense will provide its own testimony to illustrate, perhaps, that other people exercise more care when operating this type of dangerous equipment. In addition, the defense will offer testimony that the plaintiff can live a more normal life than he claims at trial.

The jury will weigh each of these competing stories to determine which account holds together better. During the client interview, the attorney must think of the potential responses and position of the adversary to each fact recounted. If inconsistencies or gaps in the account emerge, the lawyer investigates and resolves these with the client. For example, the plaintiff's lawyer might anticipate that the defense will allege inadequate preparation by the plaintiff for using a dangerous piece of equipment. Plaintiff's lawyer will therefore inquire and probe into the extent to which the plaintiff did read operating instructions and exercised caution.

The defense will likewise anticipate attacks on the adequacy of product safety. Defendants will need to ask representatives of the designer and manufacturer about safety considerations. The need for such information is reflected by the bits of evidence offered by each client and witness and following evaluation of whether each new bit of testimony fits within the overall story. Paul M. Lisnek, *Effective Client Communication: A Lawyer's Guide to Interviewing and Counseling,* West Publishing Company, St. Paul, Minnesota, 1992; sec. 5.4.

During the initial client interview, the defendant may not disclose all relevant details to the lawyer because of anxiety which leads the client to forget or block out detrimental information. The lawyer listens to the details as they are related, always with an ear towards anticipating the other side's case. The lawyer then

DEPOSITIONS: Procedures, Strategy and Techniques, designed for use in CLE programs, is the textual abridgement of the looseleaf edition which includes forms on disk. The section and form numbering from the looseleaf edition have been retained in the Professional Education Edition.

probes any cloudy or incomplete aspects of the client story to insure its overall consistency, coherence and completeness. Depositions become the tool for testing, evaluation and trial. *Id.*

§ 2.8 Competing Stories—Determining the Adversary's Position

One function of the storytelling model during each deposition is to determine the opposing counsel's competing story. The adversary's story most often contradicts the client's story or raises questions regarding the consistency, completeness or coherence of the client's story.

Lawyers cannot discover the strength of the other side's story until they first uncover the weaknesses and inconsistencies of their own client's story. Once recognizing the gaps or inconsistencies in their own client's story, lawyers can come to understand how the other party's lawyer will manipulate or exploit these weaknesses in creating a contrary version of events.

The lawyer then anticipates and prepares for potential counter attacks; this preparation involves re-evaluating the underlying facts of the case and the motivation of all parties involved. Depending upon how the lawyer comes to view the account, the client may be advised that trial is a promising avenue, or that settlement is a more viable option. Paul M. Lisnek, *Effective Client Communication: A Lawyer's Guide to Interviewing and Counseling,* West Publishing Company, St. Paul, Minnesota, 1992; sec. 5.5.

DEPOSITIONS: Procedures, Strategy and Techniques, designed for use in CLE programs, is the textual abridgement of the looseleaf edition which includes forms on disk. The section and form numbering from the looseleaf edition have been retained in the Professional Education Edition.

Form 2-1

Deposition Preparation—Deciding to Take a Deposition

Case _____ Client Name _____ File # _____

Prospective Deponent: _____

Role in Case: _____

Case Issue	What can witness prove?	Why information is important	Importance Rating	Alternative means to obtain info	Supplementary documentary proof neeeded
1.					
2.					
3.					
4.					
5.					

The above summary of case issues considered with facts proven and the issue importance rating leads me to conclude that this prospective deponent:

___ must ___ should ___ is desirable to ___ should not ___ must not be deposed.

Comments and Reasoning: _____

_____

_____

Date of last address confirmation: (To be updated every 6 months)

Source of Address: _____

___ Witness Report   ___ Telephone Directory   ___ Party Rpt
___ Dept of Motor Vehicles   ___ Other (Specify):

Corrected Address: _____

Correct as of : ____

Form 2-1
[G20,487]

A.   Name of presenting Attorney: _____

       Law Firm Name: _____

                                          _____

                                          _____

       Firm Telephone: _____

B.   Deposition Information:

       Date of Deposition: _____

       Court Reporter Service: _____

       Court Reporter: _____

       Court Reporter Telephone: _____

       Deposition ordered written? __ Yes __ No

       If yes, ordered by: _____

C.   Transcript Receipt:

       Date Reviewed _____

       Date Signed _____

       Date Filed _____

Form 2-1 (continued)
[G20,488]

Form 2-2

Deposition Record Form

Case _____ Client Name _____ File # _____

1.   Name of Party: _____

      __ Plaintiff   __ Defendant   __ Third Party Def.

      A.   Name of Presenting Attorney: _____

             Law Firm Name: _____

             Firm Address: _____

                      _____

                      _____

             Firm Telephone: _____

      B.   Deposition Information:
             Date of Deposition: _____

             Court Reporter Service: _____

             Court Reporter: _____

             Court Reporter Telephone: _____

             Deposition ordered written? __ Yes __ No

             If yes, ordered by: _____

      C.   Transcript Receipt:
             Date Reviewed ____

             Date Signed ____

             Date Filed ____

2.   Name of Witness: _____

         Favors   __ Plaintiff   __ Defendant

         Current Address: _____

         Address current as of: _____

Form 2-2
[G20,489]

Form 2-3

Storytelling Model Note–Taking Format for Depositions

Central
Common   vs.
Issue

Central
Common
Issue

Central Common Issue # 1 _____
(to which all parties agree)

Testimony on Issue			
Identity of Our Witness	Relevant Testimony	Potential Contrary Testimony	Identity of Adverse Witness

Form 2-3
[G20,490]

Central Common Issue # 2 _____
(to which all parties agree)

Testimony on Issue			
Identity of Our Witness	Relevant Testimony	Potential Contrary Testimony	Identity of Adverse Witness

Central Common Issue # 3 _____
(to which all parties agree)

Testimony on Issue			
Identity of Our Witness	Relevant Testimony	Potential Contrary Testimony	Identity of Adverse Witness

Having considered all anticipated testimony, assess the strength of the story to be presented on a scale of 1 (weak) to 10 (strong) for its:

Consistency __
Coherence __
Completeness __

Form 2-3 (continued)
[G20,491]

41

Identify the information which creates inconsistency in the story:

How to clear up the inconsistency:

Identify the aspects of the story that impede its coherence:

How to improve coherence:

Identify what is missing from the story thereby creating incompleteness:

How to obtain missing information to create a complete story:

Form 2-3 (continued)
[G20,492]

42

Form 2-4

Assessing the Story of Adverse Parties through Deposition

Using the information gathered in 2-3, create and assess the story which can be expected to be presented by adverse parties in their deposition. This information is essential to assessing one's own story for its consistency, coherence and completeness.

Summary of anticipated story of adverse party # 1:

    Response

Summary of anticipated story of adverse party # 2:

    Response

Summary of anticipated story of adverse party # 3:

    Response

Ways to create *inconsistency* in the story of the adversaries:

Ways to create *incoherence* in the story of the adversaries:

Ways to create *incompleteness* in the story of the adversaries:

Form 2-4
[G20,493]

Form 2-5

Preparation for Deposition

Case _____ Client Name _____ File # _____

1. Names of all Parties:

   Plaintiff 1: _____

       Discovery Completed:

       1. Prior Statements:

           a. Date of Statement: _____

           b. Interviewer: _____

           c. Fact Summary: _____

              _____

              _____

              _____

       2. Interrogatories Completed:

           a. Propounded by: _____

           b. Date of Filing: _____

           c. Date Responses filed: _____

           d. Information Disclosed: _____

              _____

              _____

              _____

   Plaintiff 2: _____

       Discovery Completed:

       1. Prior Statements:

           a. Date of Statement: _____

           b. Interviewer: _____

    c. Fact Summary: _____

    _____

    _____

    _____

2. Interrogatories Completed:

    a. Propounded by: _____

    b. Date of Filing: _____

    c. Date Responses filed: _____

    d. Information Disclosed: _____

    _____

    _____

    _____

Defendant # 1: _____

    Discovery Completed:

1. Prior Statements:

    a. Date of Statement: _____

    b. Interviewer: _____

    c. Fact Summary: _____

    _____

    _____

    _____

2. Interrogatories Completed:

    a. Propounded by: _____

    b. Date of Filing: _____

    c. Date Responses filed: _____

Form 2-5 (continued)
[G20,495]

45

d. Information Disclosed: _____

_____

_____

_____

Defendant # 2: _____

Discovery Completed:

1. Prior Statements:

a. Date of Statement: _____

b. Interviewer: _____

c. Fact Summary: _____

_____

_____

_____

2. Interrogatories Completed:

a. Propounded by: _____

b. Date of Filing: _____

c. Date Responses filed: _____

d. Information Disclosed: _____

_____

_____

_____

Defendant # 3: _____

Discovery Completed:

1. Prior Statements:

a. Date of Statement: _____

b. Interviewer: _____

Form 2-5 (continued)
[G20,496]

46

c. Fact Summary: _____

_____

_____

_____

2. Interrogatories Completed:

a. Propounded by: _____

b. Date of Filing: _____

c. Date Responses filed: _____

d. Information Disclosed: _____

_____

_____

_____

Third Party Defendant: _____

1. Prior Statements:

a. Date of Statement: _____

b. Interviewer: _____

c. Fact Summary: _____

_____

_____

_____

2. Interrogatories Completed:

a. Propounded by: _____

b. Date of Filing: _____

c. Date Responses filed: _____

Form 2-5 (continued)
[G20,497]

d. Information Disclosed: _____

_____

_____

_____

2. Names of all Witnesses:

a. Name: _____ Fact _____ Expert _____

Role in Case: _____

_____

_____

Discovery Completed:

1. Prior Statements:

a. Date of Statement: _____

b. Interviewer: _____

c. Fact Summary: _____

_____

_____

_____

d. Witness Completed: _____

_____

_____

2. Interrogatories Completed:

a. Propounded by: _____

b. Date of Filing: _____

c. Date Responses filed: _____

d. Information Disclosed: _____

_____

_____

Form 2-5 (continued)
[G20,498]

b. Name: _____

    Discovery Completed:

      1. Prior Statements:

          a. Date of Statement: _____

          b. Interviewer: _____

          c. Fact Summary: _____

             _____

             _____

             _____

          d. Witness Impression: _____

             _____

             _____

      2. Interrogatories Completed:

          a. Propounded by: _____

          b. Date of Filing: _____

          c. Date Responses filed: _____

          d. Information Disclosed: _____

             _____

             _____

c. Name: _____

    Discovery Completed:

      1. Prior Statements:

          a. Date of Statement: _____

          b. Interviewer: _____

          c. Fact Summary: _____

             _____

             _____

Form 2-5 (continued)
[G20,499]

49

d. Witness Impression: _____

_____

_____

2. Interrogatories Completed:

   a. Propounded by: _____

   b. Date of Filing: _____

   c. Date Responses filed: _____

   d. Information Disclosed: _____

_____

_____

Form 2-5 (continued)
[G20,500]

Deposition Preparation—Understanding Position of Self

Case _____ Client Name _____ File # _____

1. State issue: _____

    _____

    _____

2. State *your* position on the issue: _____

    _____

    _____

    _____

3. Clarify the opposing position(s) to the issue: _____

    _____

    _____

    _____

4. What known facts corroborate your position? _____

    _____

    _____

    _____

5. What known facts supplement your position? _____

    _____

    _____

    _____

6. What known facts contradict your position? _____

    _____

    _____

    _____

7. What known facts weaken your position? _____

    _____

    _____

    _____

Form 2-10
[G20,501]

51

Form 2-11

Deposition Preparation—Understanding the Position of Others

Case _____ Client Name _____ File # _____

Party Name (Other than self) _____

___ Plaintiff   ___ Defendant   ___ Third Party Def.

Party's position in the Litigation:

1.   What facts support the position? _____

       _____

       _____

2.   What facts weaken the position? _____

       _____

       _____

       _____

3.   Your opinion regarding the other's position:

       ___ Agree   ___ Disagree   ___ Neutral

       ___ It's strong   ___ It's weak   ___ Unsure

4.   Specify your desired response to the position:

       ___ Confirm it   ___ Attack it   ___ Do not investigate

5.   Steps necessary to carry out your position as specified in Questions 3 and 4: (assuring no neutral or "do not investigate" position is taken).

       a.   Depose the following individuals: (specify role in case) _____

            _____

            _____

            _____

       b.   Draft interrogatories to: _____

            _____

            Specify issues for interrogatories: _____

            _____

Form 2-11
[G20,502]

c.   Prepare request for the following documents: _____
_____

d.   Prepare requests to admit as follows: _____
_____

e.   Notice the following inspection: _____
_____

Form 2-12

Attorney Self Evaluation Sheet

1. Deposition Record

Case Name	Date	Deponent	Tactics Employed	Strong Moments	Weak Moments	Skills to Improve

2. Factor Strengths and Weaknesses

Factor	Strengths	Weaknesses
Preparation		
Legal analysis		
Attitude toward other lawyers		
Attitude toward client/witness		

3. Strengths of Personal Character: _____

_____

_____

_____

Form 2-12
[G20,504]

54

4. Areas to Improve Character: (ego, involvement, relations) _____

_____

_____

5.   Personal Reputation: (as reported by others)

Case Name	Date	Activity	Opinion	Facts

Form 2-12 (continued)
[G20,505]

Form 2-13

Opposing Attorney Evaluation Sheet

Attorney: _____

Current Firm: _____

Biographical Sketch: (education, work experience, special skills) _____

_____

_____

_____

Prior Cases with you/your office: _____

Case Name	Settlement or Verdict Amount	Performance Rating

Reputation:

Role	Strengths	Facts	Weaknesses	Facts
opposing lawyer				
co-defendant				
co-plaintiff				

Factor	Strengths	Facts	Weaknesses	Facts
legal analysis				
competency				
attitude to other lawyers				
attitude to witnesses/client preparedness				
credibility of opinion				

Form 2-13
[G20,506]

56

Tactics Employed:

Tactic	When employed	Against Whom (personality type)	Comments

Best approach to use when working *with* this attorney?

_____

_____

_____

Best approach to use when *opposing* this attorney?

_____

_____

_____

Cautions to note when *working with* this attorney:

_____

_____

_____

Cautions to note when *opposing* this attorney:

_____

_____

_____

Form 2-13 (continued)
[G20,507]

Chapter 4

MATTERS TO CONSIDER BEFORE THE DEPOSITION

Table of Sections

---

§ 4.1   Generally

After deciding to depose a witness, an attorney must satisfy various pre-deposition procedural rules. The deposing attorney must first establish a proper time and location for the deposition. The attorney then must serve notice and subpoenas. The deposing attorney also should consider who should be present at the deposition. When the time and place of the deposition have been established, the attorney should determine the best method of, and arrange for, presentation of the record.

---

§ 4.2   Timing

The federal rules generally give to counsel discretion to establish their own discovery plan and their own discovery sequence. *See e.g.,* Fed.R.Civ.P. 26(d). That discretion includes the order in which depositions are taken. Leave of court generally is not required before taking a deposition. In a lawsuit in which the parties are required to meet and confer to make initial disclosures, however, the parties typically will be unable to conduct additional discovery until they have completed that conference and made initial disclosures of relevant information. After any such required initial disclosures are made, the parties are free to conduct depositions in any sequence they deem proper. Whether or not the parties are required to meet to make initial disclosures before conducting depositions, the federal rules establish a presumptive limit of ten depositions for each "side" in the litigation. Fed.R.Civ.P. 30(a)(2)(A). In addition, the federal rules recognize eight situations in which leave of court must be obtained before a deposition can be taken.

First, under Rule 27, a person who wishes to "perpetuate testimony" regarding any lawsuit which might be filed in federal court, must, upon filing an appropriate verified petition in the district court where the proposed deponent resides, obtain leave of that court to take any deposition before the action commences.

Second, leave of court must be obtained before taking the deposition of a person confined in prison. Fed. R.Civ.P. 30(a)(2).

Third, in the absence of a written stipulation by the parties, leave of court must be obtained where a proposed deposition would result in more than ten depositions by the plaintiffs, defendants or third-party defendants. Fed.R.Civ.P. 30(a)(2)(A). This requirement is designed to impress upon counsel their professional obligation to cooperate in developing a cost-effective deposition plan in the case. *See* Ad.Gnn.Notes, Fed.R.Civ.P.

30(a)(2)(A). If the parties agree in writing to allow the plaintiffs, defendants or third-party defendants to take more than ten depositions in the case, they need not seek court-approval to do so. If, however, one party objects to an increase in the presumptive limit of ten depositions, the court must approve any additional depositions. In that circumstance, the district court has discretion, in accordance with Federal Rule 26(b)(2), to deny the request for additional depositions, or to define the terms and length of any such additional depositions. *See* Ad.Comm.Notes, Fed.R.Civ.P. 26(a)(2)(A).

Among the factors which the court should consider in deciding whether to permit a particular side to take more than 10 depositions are the cumulative nature of the testimony, the substantial need for the deposition testimony, the convenience of the parties and the deponent, the burden and expense of the deposition, the parties' resources, the amount at stake and the role of the deposition in resolving the dispute. Fed.R.Civ.P. 26(b)(2). For purposes of determining the number of depositions which have been or are proposed to be taken, a Rule 30(b)(6) deposition of an organization is treated as a single deposition, even if more than one person may be designated to testify on behalf of that organization. *See* Ad.Comm.Notes, Fed.R.Civ.P. 26(a)(2)(A).

Furthermore, because the presumptive limit of ten depositions applies to each "side," multiple parties on the same "side" of the litigation must confer and agree amongst themselves about which ten depositions they should take. If these multiple parties cannot agree on the ten depositions to be taken, a court order must be obtained to resolve their dispute or to allow additional depositions.

Fourth, a court order or written stipulation of the parties must also be obtained before any witness is deposed for the second time in the same action. Fed.R.Civ.P. 30(a)(2)(B). The Advisory Committee Notes make clear that this requirement does not apply where a deposition is merely adjourned for the convenience of the

DEPOSITIONS: Procedures, Strategy and Techniques, designed for use in CLE programs, is the textual abridgement of the looseleaf edition which includes forms on disk. The section and form numbering from the looseleaf edition have been retained in the Professional Education Edition.

parties, counsel or the deponent. Nor does it apply where the deposition is adjourned pending the production of additional requested materials relevant to the examination. Ad.Comm.Notes, Fed.R.Civ.P. 30(A)(2)(B). Nonetheless, before temporarily adjourning a deposition for any period longer than routine breaks, counsel should state clearly on the record that the deposition has not been completed, and that the adjournment is only temporary.

Fifth, as a general rule, no depositions may be taken without leave of court or agreement of the parties until after the parties have met and conferred in accordance with Federal Rule 26(f). Leave of court or stipulation is not required, however, if the notice of deposition contains a certification with supporting facts that the proposed deponent is expected to leave the United States and must be deposed promptly. Fed.R.Civ.P. 30(a)(2)(c).

Sixth, before deposing a non-testifying, consulting expert, a party must obtain a court order by showing that exceptional circumstances warrant the examination. Fed.R.Civ.P. 26(a)(4)(B). Exceptional circumstances exist where the facts or opinions held by the proposed deponents are probative of genuine issues in the case and cannot be discovered by any other means. *See* Fed.R.Civ.P. 26(a)(4)(B); 35(b)

Seventh, although leave of court is not required before deposing a testifying expert, such an expert cannot be deposed before that expert has tendered a report, as required by Federal Rule 26(a)(2)(B). Unless the parties stipulate otherwise, the expert's report generally need not be submitted until 90 days before trial. Fed. R.Civ.P. 26(a)(2)(c). Accordingly, as a practical matter, the deposition of a testifying expert will not take place until the late stages of litigation, typically within the last months before trial.

Finally, in the absence of a stipulation by the parties, leave of court must be obtained before taking a

DEPOSITIONS: Procedures, Strategy and Techniques, designed for use in CLE programs, is the textual abridgement of the looseleaf edition which includes forms on disk. The section and form numbering from the looseleaf edition have been retained in the Professional Education Edition.

deposition by telephone or other remote electronic devices such as satellite television, Fed.R.Civ.P. 30(b)(F).

§ 4.7 Notice of Oral Deposition—Generally

The typical deposition is taken orally. For these routine depositions, "reasonable notice" must be given to the deponent and every party to the action. Fed. R.Civ.P. 30(b)(1).

Reasonable notice has two components: information and time. Fed.R.Civ.P. 30(b)(1) requires that notice include the following information:

(1) place of deposition;

(2) time of deposition;

(3) deponent's name;

(4) deponent's address;

(5) a general description of deponent sufficient to identify him, if his name is not known;

(6) the materials to be produced at the deposition if a subpoena duces tecum has been served; and

(7) the method or methods by which the examiner will record the deposition, including stenography, audio tape and video tape. Fed.R.Civ.P. 30(b)(2).

The notice, however, may be imprecise regarding all of this required information. For example, the deposition can be noticed at a "mutually convenient place to be agreed to later" and can be scheduled to continue generally from day to day until completion. *See*, 8 Wright & Miller, Federal Practice and Procedure, § 2111. The deponent's name and address may be omitted if not known. Moreover, an organization may be asked to designate a deponent who is most knowledgeable to testify to certain matters. Fed.R.Civ.P. 30(b)(6). Thus, despite the formal requirements of information in the notice, the courts have allowed the parties considerable latitude to conduct discovery in a mutually beneficial and professional manner.

The Federal Rules do not contain formal requirements for the timing of notice. What constitutes a "reasonable" time will be assessed on a case-by-case basis. In the typical case with a relatively lengthy discovery period, reasonable notice is no less than five days before the examination. *See* Wright & Miller, at § 2111. But where the court has ordered expedited discovery such as in hotly contested corporate takeover litigation, "reasonable" notice becomes a period of hours.

Whether notice is vague or precise, relaxed or expedited, the standard of reasonableness will be informed by the over-arching goals of the Federal Rules. These Rules are designed to foster the just and efficient resolution of disputes based upon their merits, rather than upon hypertechnical rules of pleading. *See* Fed.R.Civ.P. 1. Meritorious dispute resolution requires the clash of two prepared adversaries. Thus, deposition notice is reasonable under the Federal Rules if it affords the deponent an opportunity to prepare for the deposition and the deponent's attorney an opportunity to prepare to question the witness.

§ 4.8 Notice to Party Deponents

Reasonable notice given to a party pursuant to Fed.R.Civ.P. 5 is generally sufficient to compel the party's attendance at the deposition. The failure of the party to attend his deposition will result in the sanctions of Fed.R.Civ.P. 37(b)(2)(A), (B), and (C). Those sanctions include: an order that facts adverse to the non-appearing deponent be admitted, prohibiting the non-appearing deponent from introducing certain evidence, striking claims or defenses, staying proceedings, or dismissing the action. The court also has discretion to sanction non-attendance by entering any other order it deems just or awarding appropriate attorneys fees.

Moreover, under Fed.R. of Civ.P. 30(b)(5) notice to a party which includes a request made in compliance with Fed.R.Civ.P. 34 for the production of documents is sufficient to compel that production. The Advisory Committee Notes to Fed.R.Civ.P. 30(b)(5) caution that where the documents requested are "many and complex," the deponent may seek a court order that productions be accomplished under the traditional Fed.R.Civ.P. 34 procedures. The notice of deposition to an individual party can and should include a request to bring to the deposition those documents which are "closely related to the oral examination." Adv.Comm. Notes, Fed.R.Civ.P. 30(b)(5). Forms 4–4 and 4–5 are examples of sufficient notice to an individual and organizational party.

§ 4.9 Notice to Non-party Deponents and Subpoenas

When the deponent is not a party, the sanctions of Fed.R.Civ.P. 37(d) are inadequate to compel deposition attendance. A subpoena must issue to compel the attendance of a non-party witness. The fact that a subpoena is issued, however, does not relieve the deposing party of the duty to provide reasonable notice to every other party to the action. See Fed.R.Civ.P. 30(b)(1). Hence, when a non-party is to be deposed, the deposing party must both serve a subpoena on the deponent and provide notice.

Under Federal Rule 45, a subpoena compelling the attendance of a witness at a deposition must be issued by the court in the district where the deposition is to be taken. The subpoena may include a command that the witness bring evidence to the deposition. Fed.R.Civ.P. 45(a)(1). In that situation, the district court where the deposition is to be taken may issue a subpoena for both the attendance of the witness and the production of evidence. Alternatively, two separate subpoenas may be issued, one compelling attendance at a deposition and the other compelling the production of evidence. In that situation, however, the separate subpoena for the production of evidence must be issued by the district court in which the production is to be made. Fed.R.Civ.P. 45(a)(2).

DEPOSITIONS: Procedures, Strategy and Techniques, designed for use in CLE programs, is the textual abridgement of the looseleaf edition which includes forms on disk. The section and form numbering from the looseleaf edition have been retained in the Professional Education Edition.

Every subpoena must contain the following:

1. The name of the court from which it is issued;
2. The title of the action;
3. The name of the court in which the action is pending;
4. The civil action number;
5. A command to each person to whom it is directed to attend and give testimony and/or to produce evidence or permit inspection of evidence in that person's possession, custody or control, and
6. The text of Fed.R.Civ.P. 45(c) and (d) which provides:

   (c) **Protection of Persons Subject to Subpoenas.**

       (1) A party or an attorney responsible for the issuance and service of a subpoena shall take reasonable steps to avoid imposing undue burden or expense on a person subject to that subpoena. The court on behalf of which the subpoena was issued shall enforce this duty and impose upon the party or attorney in breach of this duty an appropriate sanction, which may include, but is not limited to, lost earnings and a reasonable attorney's fee.

       (2)(A) A person commanded to produce and permit inspection and copying of designated books, papers, documents or tangible things, or inspection of premises need not appear in person at the place of production or inspection unless commanded to appear for deposition, hearing or trial.

       (B) Subject to paragraph (d)(2) of this rule, a person commanded to produce and permit inspection and copying may, within 14 days after service of the subpoena or before the time specified for compliance if such time is less than 14 days after service, serve upon the party or attorney designated in the subpoena written objec-

DEPOSITIONS: Procedures, Strategy and Techniques, designed for use in CLE programs, is the textual abridgement of the looseleaf edition which includes forms on disk. The section and form numbering from the looseleaf edition have been retained in the Professional Education Edition.

tion to inspection or copying of any or all of the designated materials or of the premises. If objection is made, the party serving the subpoena shall not be entitled to inspect and copy the materials or inspect the premises except pursuant to an order of the court by which the subpoena was issued. If objection has been made, the party serving the subpoena may, upon notice to the person commanded to produce, move at any time for an order to compel the production. Such an order to compel production shall protect any person who is not a party or an officer of a party from significant expense resulting from the inspection and copying commanded.

(3)(A) On timely motion, the court by which a subpoena was issued shall quash or modify the subpoena if it

   (i) fails to allow reasonable time for compliance;

   (ii) requires a person who is not a party or an officer of a party to travel to a place more than 100 miles from the place where that person resides, is employed or regularly transacts business in person, except that, subject to the provisions of clause (c)(3)(B)(iii) of this rule, such a person may in order to attend trial be commanded to travel from any such place within the state in which the trial is held, or

   (iii) requires disclosure of privileged or other protected matter and no exception or waiver applies, or

   (iv) subjects a person to undue burden.

DEPOSITIONS: Procedures, Strategy and Techniques, designed for use in CLE programs, is the textual abridgement of the looseleaf edition which includes forms on disk. The section and form numbering from the looseleaf edition have been retained in the Professional Education Edition.

(B) If a subpoena

(i) requires disclosure of a trade secret or other confidential research, development, or commercial information, or

(ii) requires disclosure of an unretained expert's opinion or information not describing specific events or occurrences in dispute and resulting from the expert's study made not at the request of any party, or

(iii) requires a person who is not a party or an officer of a party to incur substantial expense to travel more than 100 miles to attend trial, the court may, to protect a person subject to or affected by the subpoena, quash or modify the subpoena or, if the party in whose behalf the subpoena is issued shows a substantial need for the testimony or material that cannot be otherwise met without undue hardship and assures that the person to whom the subpoena is addressed will be reasonably compensated, the court may order appearance or production only upon specified conditions.

(d) **Duties in Responding to Subpoena.**

(1) A person responding to a subpoena to produce documents shall produce them as they are kept in the usual course of business or shall organize and label them to correspond with the categories in the demand.

(2) When information subject to a subpoena is withheld on a claim that it is privileged or subject to protection as trial preparation materials, the claim shall be made expressly and shall be

DEPOSITIONS: Procedures, Strategy and Techniques, designed for use in CLE programs, is the textual abridgement of the looseleaf edition which includes forms on disk. The section and form numbering from the looseleaf edition have been retained in the Professional Education Edition.

> supported by a description of the nature of the documents, communications, or things not produced that is sufficient to enable the demanding party to contest the claim.

The subpoena may be issued by the clerk upon the request of a party. But more significantly, an attorney, as an officer of the court may issue and sign a subpoena if that attorney is authorized to practice in the court where the action is pending. Fed.R.Civ.P. 45(a)(3). Under these liberalized provisions, attorneys may obtain blank subpoenas from the clerk of courts and simply issue them at their convenience.

§ 4.11 Location—Generally

Attorneys should select the best location for the deposition that the rules will allow. Accordingly, the attorney must first determine which geographical locations are proper. Then, the attorney should decide which of the proper geographic locations is the best strategic location. Finally, attorneys must select an optimal site within that geographic location. Form 4–3 provides a vehicle for analyzing each of these concerns.

§ 4.12 Proper Location

The Federal Rules governing depositions do not require that they be held in any specific location. Fed. R.Civ.P. 45 governs subpoenas for taking depositions and does limit the reach of those subpoenas. A non-party upon whom a deposition subpoena has been served generally cannot be required to attend the deposition at any place greater than 100 miles from the place where he resides, is employed or transacts business.

The question of proper deposition location, therefore, hinges on whether a Fed.R.Civ.P. 45 subpoena must be served. The Federal Rules do not require that a subpoena be served, even as to non-party deponents. Hence, it is possible to take the deposition of parties and non-parties in any geographic location. It is not possible, however, to *compel* the attendance of a non-party witness at a deposition without a subpoena. Fed. R.Civ.P. 37(d) provides its own sanctions for a *party's* failure to attend at his own deposition. The sanctions, the most severe of which is default, however, are discretionary and difficult to obtain. This Rule also provides sanctions for the failure of a party's agent, director, managing agent or testifying agent to appear at deposition. This Rule does not, however, provide any sanction for the failure of a person other than a party, or its officer, director, managing agent or testifying agent to appear at a deposition. Accordingly, the attendance of such a person can only be compelled by a Fed.R.Civ.P. 45 subpoena. The sanction for failing to comply with a subpoena is contempt (Fed.R.Civ.P. 45(e)) and can be avoided only if there is an "adequate excuse" such as an *inability* to comply.

Together, the Federal Rules suggest the following location guidelines:

1. The deposition of a party can be held in any geographic location because the nonattendance of the party can be sanctioned under Fed. R.Civ.P. 37(d).

2. Because a person not a party or officer, director, managing agent or testifying agent of a party cannot be compelled to appear at a deposition without a subpoena and because the subpoena requires the deposition to be taken within 100 miles of that person's residence, business, employment, attorneys should serve such a subpoena and fix the deposition location within those boundaries.

Although a Fed.R.Civ.P. 45(d) subpoena is not needed to compel a party's attendance at a deposition, attorneys should nevertheless consider issuing one. The subpoena's contempt sanction adds teeth to Fed.R.Civ.P. 37(d) sanctions.

DEPOSITIONS: Procedures, Strategy and Techniques, designed for use in CLE programs, is the textual abridgement of the looseleaf edition which includes forms on disk. The section and form numbering from the looseleaf edition have been retained in the Professional Education Edition.

Whether attendance has been compelled pursuant to notice or subpoena, the Rules allow the prospective deponent to attempt a change in the deposition's location. Fed.R.Civ.P. 26(c)(2) empowers the court to enter a protective order, setting the place of discovery. Further, the court may modify the place of deposition in response to a motion to quash the subpoena. The court has wide discretion to fix the place of deposition, so long as the motion for a protective order or to quash the subpoena is made seasonably.

In exercising its discretion, the district court will be guided by these presumptions: the plaintiff should be available for deposition in the district where the suit was filed and a defendant corporation should be deposed at its principal place of business. *See* Wright & Miller, 8 Federal Practice and Procedure, § 2112. Apart from these presumptions, courts weigh the financial hardship to both parties in deciding to alter location, and have on occasion required the payment of travel expenses. *Id.; see also* Thompson v. Sun Oil Co., 523 F.2d 647 (8th Cir.1975).

Although the Rules favor attorneys traveling great distances to take depositions, the current practice is for attorneys to offer to pay deponents to come to their offices. An attorney's travel time at an hourly rate can be much more expensive to the client than the cost of a witness's travel expenses alone.

§ 4.13 Strategic Location

After the attorney has determined which locations comport with the discovery rules, he should decide which location affords the greatest strategic advantage. Common sense dictates that the deposition be noticed at a location most convenient for the deposing attorney and the client, and least convenient for the adversary. Yet, such a strategy is not only counterproductive, it is subject to sanction. The court's power to enter a protective order will be used to block a deponent's gross inconvenience or expense. Moreover, Fed.R.Civ.P. 11 provides

DEPOSITIONS: Procedures, Strategy and Techniques, designed for use in CLE programs, is the textual abridgement of the looseleaf edition which includes forms on disk. The section and form numbering from the looseleaf edition have been retained in the Professional Education Edition.

70

sanctions for the use of discovery to "needlessly increase the cost of litigation." Thus, while it may be common practice for attorneys to beat impecunious adversaries into submission with burdensome discovery requests, such as a distant deposition, this practice violates the Federal Rules.

Rather than attempt to inconvenience the adversary, therefore, attorneys selecting a site for the deposition should ensure the convenience of their own clients. The deposition location, therefore, should be at a reasonable, and *mutually* agreeable place. Where a deposition of the attorney's client is contemplated for the future, the agreement should include a contingency that the future deposition also take place at a mutually convenient place. The location of a deposition clearly becomes a strategic bargaining tool for the course of discovery.

§ 4.14   The Deposition Site—Local

The deposition should be noticed at a place familiar and comfortable to the deposing attorney. Naturally, the deposing attorney's offices are the best place to depose a witness. When the deposition is at the deposing attorney's office, he can reserve a conference room, meet the court reporter and create a "seating chart" for all the participants before the deponent even arrives. He has ready access to additional files and to the advice of colleagues. He also has the ability to use phones and additional offices without fear of losing confidentiality.

The only negative aspect to deposing a witness in one's own office is the access given the adverse attorneys to that office. In a large case where several firm attorneys work on the matter which is the subject of the deposition, it is not uncommon for the adversary's attorneys to overhear the host firm's unsuspecting attorneys talking freely of the case in the nearby firm library or corridors. Attorneys may leave a revealing file in places where it can be viewed by the adversary's attorneys, an inadvertent disclosure having disastrous consequences. Accordingly, any time a deposition (or any other meet-

DEPOSITIONS: Procedures, Strategy and Techniques, designed for use in CLE programs, is the textual abridgement of the looseleaf edition which includes forms on disk. The section and form numbering from the looseleaf edition have been retained in the Professional Education Edition.

ing) is to take place in an office, the entire office must be cautioned that the adversary's attorneys will be present. So long as requisite care is taken, an attorney's own office provides the optimal strategic location for a deposition.

§ 4.15 Deposition Site—Out-of-Town

If the deposition must be taken out-of-town, the deposing attorney should try to use the law offices of an attorney with whom he is familiar. Attorneys often accommodate their out-of-town colleagues by providing conference rooms for deposition. The accommodation is reciprocated in kind. Co-counsel in current or prior cases are likely candidates for this accommodation, as are longstanding colleagues of the firm or frequent referral sources. In order to obtain the possible sources of accommodation, a deposing attorney should circulate an intraoffice memorandum well in advance of the deposition which solicits source names, addresses and phone numbers.

In the unfortunate situation where no law office site out-of-town is available, attorneys frequently hold depositions in a hotel room. If the deposition must be held in a hotel, the deposing attorney should reserve one of the hotel's meeting rooms. The meeting room should contain a telephone, writing materials and beverages. Taking a deposition in a hotel meeting room is vastly superior to taking a deposition in a small hotel room. A deposition taken in a dark, cramped hotel room across twin-beds makes for a great war story, but also makes for a bad deposition. The deposing attorney should insist that the deposition take place in a comfortable, well-supplied and formal room.

§ 4.16 Persons Attending the Deposition

Depositions are not generally considered open proceedings for public attendance. Seattle Times Co. v. Rhinehart, 467 U.S. 20, 33, 104 S.Ct. 2199, 2208, 81

DEPOSITIONS: Procedures, Strategy and Techniques, designed for use in CLE programs, is the textual abridgement of the looseleaf edition which includes forms on disk. The section and form numbering from the looseleaf edition have been retained in the Professional Education Edition.

L.Ed.2d 17 (1984). The following individuals may be present during the deposition:

(1) *The deponent.* Whether a party, witness or other non-party, any person who has information deemed relevant to the issues in a litigation is subject to deposition.

(2) *Attorney representing the deponent.* This attorney, if representing the party or retained by a non-party, has the right to monitor the propriety and direction of the proceedings through the use of objections.

(3) *The examining or deposing attorney.* This attorney represents a party to the litigation and is usually the one who noticed the deposition thereby taking the lead in questioning.

(4) *Other party attorneys.* Any party to the litigation has a right to have an attorney present at every deposition for the purpose of uncovering information relevant to their client's role in the litigation.

(5) *The court reporter.* A certified reporter, or notary public, administers the oath to the deponent and records all testimony in writing for subsequent transcription.

(6) *The parties to the litigation.* Any party has a right to be present at all depositions. The court may exercise discretion to limit the attendance of a party, through a protective order under Fed.R.Civ.P. 26, but it is rare for a judge to prevent a party from attending any deposition. But see Galella v. Onassis, 487 F.2d 986, 997 (2d Cir.1973) where a trial judge excluded the plaintiff photographer from Jacqueline Onassis's deposition. The presence of a party at deposition is a strategic move which can serve to intimidate the deponent; conversely, a party's presence may assist the deponent to recall and state his testimony.

(7) *Non-party attendance.* Whether other persons can attend a deposition is unclear. Fed.R.Civ.P. 26(c)(5) permits the issuance of a protective order so as to permit a deposition to proceed "with no one present except

DEPOSITIONS: Procedures, Strategy and Techniques, designed for use in CLE programs, is the textual abridgement of the looseleaf edition which includes forms on disk. The section and form numbering from the looseleaf edition have been retained in the Professional Education Edition.

persons designated by the court." *Implied* by the rule is the suggestion that anyone may attend the proceedings unless precluded by protective order.

Protective orders are most likely to be sought against members of the media. In Seattle Times Co. v. Rhinehart, 467 U.S. 20, 104 S.Ct. 2199, 81 L.Ed.2d 17 (1984), however, the Supreme Court concluded that a deposition is less than a public proceeding. Unlike a trial, depositions are set for a time convenient to the attorneys and parties involved; they are not designed to meet the needs of the general public. Reality and practicality dictate that a judge will exercise discretion to restrict attendance by third persons if so requested by one of the attorneys.

Theoretically, there are few instances when a third party needs to be in attendance at a deposition. One clear conflict, however, would be an attorney who wants an expert witness present during the deposition of the opposing party's expert witness. The examiner's own expert can provide information and advice to assist in question development during the deposition; such assistance may be seen by a judge as being beyond the scope of propriety. Nevertheless, absent a protective order, no case law to date specifically restricts the presence of any third party beyond the media. Recall that Fed.R.Civ.P. 26(c)(5) requires a showing of good cause for a protective order to issue. The need to protect a patent or trade secret are examples of when restricting attendance can be desirable.

Federal Rule of Civil Procedure 26(c)(5) allows the court to order that a deposition be taken with no one present except those persons designated by the court. Some courts have analogized such an order to a "protective order" and have decided that public access to the pretrial discovery process must be afforded absent a showing of compelling reasons for denial of access. *See e.g.,* American Tel. & Tel. Co. v. Grady, 594 F.2d 594 (7th Cir.1978). More recent decisions, however, have upheld a district court's broad discretion to deny anyone

DEPOSITIONS: Procedures, Strategy and Techniques, designed for use in CLE programs, is the textual abridgement of the looseleaf edition which includes forms on disk. The section and form numbering from the looseleaf edition have been retained in the Professional Education Edition.

access to a deposition, even absent a showing of "good cause." *See e.g.,* Kimberlin v. Quinlan, 145 F.R.D. 1, 2 (D.D.C.1992). These courts reason that, "depositions and interrogatories are not public components of a civil trial." *See* Kimberlin, 145 F.R.D. at 1 (citing Seattle Times Co. v. Rhinehart, 467 U.S. 20, 33, 104 S.Ct. 2199, 2208, 81 L.Ed.2d 17 (1984); In re Reporters Comm. For Freedom of the Press, et al., 773 F.2d 1325, 1338 (D.C.Cir.1985)). As a general rule, neither "the public nor representatives of the press have a right to be present at the taking of a deposition." 8 Wright & Miller, Federal Practice and Procedure § 2041 (1993 Supp.). *See also* Grundberg v. Upjohn Co., 140 F.R.D. 459, 466 (D.Utah 1991). *But see* 15 U.S.C.A. § 30 (1970) & (1992 Supp.) (the Sherman Act contains an express provision opening depositions to the public in antitrust actions brought by the United States).

In attempting to convince the judge to deny various persons access to the deposition process, litigants must show that the presence of those persons would (1) jeopardize the confidentiality of testimony or documents revealed at the deposition; (2) "significantly hinder the discovery process,"; or (3) "burden the courts with increased litigation over discovery issues." *See, e.g.,* Kimberlin, 145 F.R.D. at 2; Beacon v. R.N. Jones Apartment Rentals, 79 F.R.D. 141 (N.D.Ohio 1978); Metal Foil Products Mfg. Co. v. Reynolds Metals Co., 55 F.R.D. 491 (E.D.Va.1970). In arguing that the court should grant access to the deposition process, litigants should attempt to show that the presence of the person or persons would (1) assist the witness to remember relevant facts or (2) assist the examining attorney in understanding expert or otherwise complex testimony. *See, e.g.,* Avirgan v. Hull, 118 F.R.D. 252 (D.D.C.1987); Dunlap v. Reading Co., 30 F.R.D. 129, 131–132 (E.D.Pa. 1962).

If any party or nonparty deponent anticipates that the attendance of various persons at an upcoming deposition will be controversial, that party or nonparty depo-

---

DEPOSITIONS: Procedures, Strategy and Techniques, designed for use in CLE programs, is the textual abridgement of the looseleaf edition which includes forms on disk. The section and form numbering from the looseleaf edition have been retained in the Professional Education Edition.

75

nent should seek an order banning those various persons from the deposition under Rule 26(c)(5).

§ 4.18 Persons Before Whom Depositions May Be Taken

The process of preparing for a deposition includes the selection of a court reporter or person before whom the deposition may be taken. The person must be both qualified and reliable.

Depositions within the United States may be taken before:

1. an officer authorized by federal law to administer oaths;

2. an officer authorized by the law of the place where the deposition is taken to administer oaths;

3. a person appointed by the court in which the action is pending; or

4. any person provided for by the parties in a written stipulation. *See* Fed.R.Civ.P. 28(a), 29.

These persons are empowered both to administer oaths and to take testimony.

The person selected to administer oaths and take testimony may, however, be disqualified for interest. The Rules provide that no deposition shall be taken before a person who is:

1. a relative of any party;

2. an employee of any party;

3. an attorney for any party;

4. a relative of an attorney of any party;

5. an employee of an attorney of any party; or

6. financially interested in the action.

See Fed.R.Civ.P. 28(c).

Although the Rules suggest that a court reporter employed by an attorney may be subject to disqualifica-

---

DEPOSITIONS: Procedures, Strategy and Techniques, designed for use in CLE programs, is the textual abridgement of the looseleaf edition which includes forms on disk. The section and form numbering from the looseleaf edition have been retained in the Professional Education Edition.

tion, they have never been construed so strictly. Attorneys should ensure that the court reporter whom they have chosen has cleared any conflicts check.

Objections to the disqualifying interest of a person before whom the deposition will be taken can be waived. The objection must be made either before the deposition begins or as soon thereafter as the grounds for the objection become known or could be discovered with reasonable diligence. Fed.R.Civ.P. 30(c); 32(d)(2). Failure to make a seasonable objection constitutes a waiver. Moreover, while the Rule mandates that a deposition not be taken before a person with a disqualifying interest, the parties may agree, by written stipulation, that the deposition be taken before such a person. Fed.R.Civ.P. 29.

In addition to being qualified, the person selected to record the deposition should be reliable. Attorneys should select a familiar, competent, cost-effective reporting service. Most reporting services respond to firm loyalty with group rates or bulk discounts. The loyalty is also rewarded by excellent service and, in some cases, special attention. Such attention is particularly helpful when a transcript is needed on an expedited basis or when extra copies of exhibits are required. Finally, there is some tactical advantage to taking a deposition before a familiar reporter; it may create the impression to the adversary that depositions are a routine part of your practice and expertise.

§ 4.19 Methods of Recording Deposition

A deposition must be recorded. *See* Fed.R.Civ.P. 30(c). Further, absent an agreement between the parties, a deposition must be recorded by the officer who administers the oath, or someone acting under the officer's direction. Fed.R.Civ.P. 30(c). Unless the court orders otherwise, a deposition may be recorded by sound, sound-and-visual, or stenographic means. Fed.R.Civ.P. 30(b)(2). The notice of deposition must indicate which method or methods the examining attorney will employ to record the deposition. Fed.R.Civ.P. 30(b)(2). The other parties in the action may upon prior notice designate additional methods of recording the deposition. Fed.R.Civ.P. 30(b)(3). A court reporter, who is authorized to administer oaths, also typically transcribes the oral examination. As a consequence, most depositions result in written transcripts. They record only the audible utterances of the examiner, deponent and attorneys. Naturally, the quality of the record is only as good as the quality of the reporter. Some reporters transcribe every utterance—including verbal pauses such as "uh, um, ah." Others, however, edit such utterances from the final transcript. Still other reporters place their own gloss on the transcription in a well-intentioned effort to have the testimony make sense. But all court reporters will miss a key word or err from time to time. No court reporter can put into writing either the demeanor of the deponent or the non-verbal component of the interaction. Thus, stenography is an imperfect, though familiar, method of recording a deposition.

In keeping with technological advances in recording devices, the Rules encourage attorneys to record depositions by other than stenographic means. Fed.R.Civ.P. 30(b)(2).

The alternative methods of recording include motion picture, tape recorder and videotape. Moreover, the Federal Rules specifically allow the parties to stipulate to any other method of taking a deposition, including telephone. Fed.R.Civ.P. 30(b)(7).

Videotape is currently the most frequently used alternative to stenography. Videotape records both the audible utterances and the non-verbal cues of the deponent. It can pick up the demeanor of the witness, and can reveal non-verbal cues given to the witness by the examiner or defending attorney. The videotaped deposition has the additional advantage at trial of being less boring to a jury than the reading of page after page of a deposition transcript.

DEPOSITIONS: Procedures, Strategy and Techniques, designed for use in CLE programs, is the textual abridgement of the looseleaf edition which includes forms on disk. The section and form numbering from the looseleaf edition have been retained in the Professional Education Edition.

Form 1A. Notice of Lawsuit and Request for Waiver of Service of Summons

TO: _____ (A) _____
    [as _____ (B) _____ of _____ (C) _____]

A lawsuit has been commenced against you (or the entity on whose behalf you are addressed). A copy of the complaint is attached to this notice. It has been filed in the United States District Court for the _____ (D) _____ and has been assigned docket number _ _____ (E) _____ .

This is not a formal summons or notification from the court, but rather my request is that you sign and return the enclosed waiver of service in order to save the cost of serving you with a judicial summons and an additional copy of the complaint. The cost of service will be avoided if I receive a signed copy of the waiver within ___ (F) ___ days after the date designated below as the date on which this Notice and request is sent. I enclose a stamped and addressed envelope (or other means of cost-free return) for your use. An extra copy of the waiver is also attached for your records.

If you comply with this request and return the signed waiver, it will be filed with the court and no summons will be served on you. The action will then proceed as if you had been served on the date the waiver is filed, except that you will not be obligated to answer the complaint before 60 days from the date designated below as the date on which this notice is sent (or before 90 days from that date if your address is not in any judicial district of the United States).

If you do not return the signed waiver within the time indicated, I will take appropriate steps to effect formal service in a manner authorized by the Federal Rules of Civil Procedure and will then, to the extent authorized by those Rules, ask the court to require you (or the party on whose behalf you are addressed) to pay the full costs of such service. In that connection, please read the statement concerning the duty of parties to waive the service of the summons, which is set forth on the reverse side (or at the foot) of the waiver form.

I affirm this request is being sent to you on behalf of the plaintiff, this ___ day of _____, ___.

_____
Signature of Plaintiff's Attorney or
Unrepresented Plaintiff

Notes:
    A—Name of individual defendant (or name of officer or agent of corporate defendant)
    B—Title, or other relationship of individual to corporate defendant
    C—Name of corporate defendant, if any
    D—District
    E—Docket number of action
    F—Addressee must be given at least 30 days (60 days if located in foreign country) in which to return waiver

Form 4-1
[G20,508]

Form 4-3

Proper Deposition Locations

Deponent	Party or Officer, Director, Managing Agent or Testify-ing Agent	Notice Non-Party	Subpoena Served	Rule 45 Served	Residence	Business	Employ	Service	Deposition Locations

Form 4-3
[G20,509]

80

Form 4-4

Notice of Deposition to Locations

_____
)
Plaintiff   )
)
              v.   )   No._____
Defendant   )
_____   )

NOTICE OF ORAL DEPOSITION OF _____

    PLEASE TAKE NOTICE that the oral deposition of _____ will be taken in accordance with Federal Rule of Civil Procedure 30 [*State Rule of Procedure*_____] at the offices of _ _____, on _____, 19__, beginning at _____ and continuing from day to day until completion. The deposition will be recorded by [*stenographic, audio or audio-visual*] methods.

    The witness is requested to bring to the deposition the documents described on the attached page.

                              _____
                                        [*Signature*]

Form 4-4
[G20,510]

Form 4-5

Notice of Oral Deposition of Organization Party

```
_____  )
                             )
Plaintiff                    )
                             )
             v.              )        No._____
                             )
Defendant                    )
                             )
_____  )
```

NOTICE OF ORAL DEPOSITION OF _____

PLEASE TAKE NOTICE that the oral deposition of _____ will be taken pursuant to Federal Rule of Civil Procedure 30(b)(6) at the offices of _____, on _____, 19__, beginning at _____ and continuing from day to day until completion.

The matters on which the examination is requested include _____

_____

_____.

In accordance with Fed.R.Civ.P. 30(b)(6), _____ shall designate officers, directors or agents to testify on its behalf as to matters known or reasonably available to _____.

The witness or witnesses designated by _____ shall bring to the deposition the document described on the attached page.

_____
[*Signature*]

Author's Comment

The standards for proper notice to depose a corporate or association party contain additional requirements. Federal Rule of Civil Procedure 30(b)(6) allows the deposing party to name as the deponent a corporation, partnership, governmental agency or other association. In doing so, however, the deposing party should "designate with reasonable particularity matters on which examination is requested." When the deponent is a non-party, this designation is compulsory. The burden then shifts to the named organization to designate persons to testify on its behalf as to matters presumptively within the knowledge of the organization. Fed.R.Civ.P. 30(b)(6). The above form provides sufficient notice for a Rule 30(b)(6) deposition.

Form 4-5
[G20,511]

Deposition Subpoena—Individual

_____)	
Plaintiff)	
v.) No._____	
Defendant)	
_____)	

TO: _____

     YOU ARE COMMANDED to appear at: _____ on _____ at _____ to testify at the taking of a deposition in the above action pending in the United States District Court for the _____, and to produce at the deposition the documents listed on the attached page.

     Dated _____, 19__.

                           By _____
                                       District Clerk

Form 4-7

Deposition Subpoena — Organization

```
_____
                             )
Plaintiff                    )
                  v.         )        No._____
Defendant                    )
                             )
_____)
```

TO: _____

YOU ARE COMMANDED to appear at: _____ on _____ at _____ to testify at the taking of a deposition in the above action pending in the United States District Court for the _____, and to produce at the deposition the documents listed on the attached page.

Pursuant to Federal Rule of Civil Procedure 30(b)(6), _____ shall file a designation with the court specifying one or more officers, directors, agents to testify regarding matters known or reasonably known to _____.

Dated _____, 19__.

By _____
   District Clerk

Chapter 5

VIDEOTAPED DEPOSITIONS

Table of Sections

---

§ 5.1 The Trend Toward Presumptive Videotaping

Federal Rule 30(b) allows the examining party to record deposition testimony by videotape without a court order to do so. Moreover, if the examining party has not indicated in the notice of deposition that the deposition will be videotaped, any other party may videotape the deposition upon proper notice. Fed.R.Civ.P. 30(b)(3). The federal rule effectively allows any party to videotape any deposition, unless the court orders otherwise.

The Rule is in keeping with the trend throughout the state courts to allow any party to record a deposition by videotape, even without approval of the court or the adversary. In light of these developments, videotaped depositions rapidly are becoming the rule rather than the exception in civil litigation. The effective use of videotape thus has become a key ingredient in an effective deposition.

§ 5.2 The Systemic Advantages and Disadvantages of Videotaping

The trend toward a presumption favoring video-taped depositions in federal and state court was borne of

---

DEPOSITIONS: Procedures, Strategy and Techniques, designed for use in CLE programs, is the textual
abridgement of the looseleaf edition which includes forms on disk. The section and form numbering
from the looseleaf edition have been retained in the Professional Education Edition.

tremendous study and debate. Court reporters and ste-
nographers, not surprisingly, stressed the disadvantages
of videotaping. But, ultimately, the advantages were
perceived to outweigh the disadvantages.

A videotaped deposition is thought to be more accurate than a stenographic deposition. A traditional deposition which is recorded stenographically and then transcribed cannot capture nonverbal communication. Yet,
a great deal of communication is nonverbal. Everyone
communicates with eye-contact, posture, gestures, facial
expressions, body position, and even clothing style. In
the deposition context, skillful attorneys exploit nonverbal communication to gain responses from the witness. In the stenographic deposition, nonverbal communication is not recorded unless it is articulated and
transcribed.

To the extent that nonverbal communication is
nonetheless communication relevant to the questioning
and answering process, a court reporter cannot capture
that communication. If the goal of recording a deposition is to capture and preserve the full range of interaction and communication during the deposition, then
videotaping clearly is more accurate than stenography.

Nonverbal communication appears to play a critical
role in a factfinder's perception of a witness' credibility.
Smiling, head-nodding, eye-movement, blinking, hand-
movements, shifting posture and speaking speeds all
tend to be perceived by jurors as indicia that the witness
is not being candid. Each of those nonverbal cues will
not be absorbed by a stenographer, but can be detected
on videotape.

Moreover, videotape can reflect a lack of harmony
between a deponent's verbal response and his or her
nonverbal movements. When a witness answers a question "yes," a court reporter can only record the signifier
"yes." But there are many different shades of "yes."
The witness may offer a defiant yes, a sarcastic yes, a
thoughtful yes, a quick yes, a deliberate yes, an annoyed

DEPOSITIONS: Procedures, Strategy and Techniques, designed for use in CLE programs, is the textual
abridgement of the looseleaf edition which includes forms on disk. The section and form numbering
from the looseleaf edition have been retained in the Professional Education Edition.

yes, or a disinterested yes. These shades of meaning can be communicated by videotape. Fact-finders thus are able to assess the credibility of the witness' testimony based on all available methods of human understanding. They can assess the witness' demeanor and credibility as if that witness were offering live testimony. Plainly, a videotaped deposition is more like live testimony than is a stenographically transcribed deposition.

Further, jurors are more likely to be influenced by a video presentation than a deposition transcript. Jurors remember what they see and hear more than what they merely read. Videotape tends to capture and hold the attention of a jury. A deposition transcript, by contrast, can be quite boring. Jurors who are used to television as a medium of communication tend to be comfortable with the presence of a television screen in the courtroom.

Videotaped depositions also permit the logical and effective presentation of out-of-court testimony. In an effort to make an otherwise dull deposition transcript come to life, attorneys often "role play" the questions and answers from a deposition transcript at trial. They might use members of their firm or their support staff to play various parts in front of the jury. They act out the deposition as if it were a screenplay. This process is extremely awkward. It is plainly artificial. It is confusing. And it can be counterproductive when attorneys are forced to play the role of the adversary's counsel in order to read questions or statements made by that counsel during the deposition. This bizarre ritual is not necessary if the deposition has been videotaped.

Finally, and perhaps most significantly, a videotape deposition captures the verbal and nonverbal testimony of witnesses who might not otherwise be available, and hence seen, at trial. Witnesses are not always available for trial. They may be outside of the court's subpoena power. They may become ill or die. In addition, friendly witnesses, such as experts, may develop scheduling conflicts which preclude them from being in court on the

DEPOSITIONS: Procedures, Strategy and Techniques, designed for use in CLE programs, is the textual abridgement of the looseleaf edition which includes forms on disk. The section and form numbering from the looseleaf edition have been retained in the Professional Education Edition.

day or at the time they are called to testify. Videotaping the deposition insures that if a witness cannot testify at trial, the fact-finder nonetheless will be able to hear and see the witness' testimony in a logical and persuasive order.

Videotaped depositions, however, are not without perceived disadvantages. Many attorneys believe that stenographic deposition are cheaper, easier to schedule, and easier to use in court than are videotaped depositions. Still other attorneys feel that deponents are more nervous in a videotaped deposition than they are in a stenographic deposition. Some attorneys no doubt fear that their well-honed stenographic deposition tactical skills will become obsolete in the video setting. Certainly, preparation for a videotaped deposition differs from that of a stenographic deposition. For some, "retraining" in this context is a disadvantage of videotaped depositions.

§ 5.3 Tactical Advantages and Disadvantages of Videotaping Depositions

Attorneys may not have a choice as to whether or not to videotape a deposition. Under the federal rules, any party may videotape a deposition without the consent of any other party or of the court. *See* Fed.R.Civ.P. 30(b)(3). The examining attorney therefore must be prepared to conduct a videotape deposition, even if that attorney does not want to conduct such an examination.

Examining attorneys, however, still must determine whether they should affirmatively designate the deposition as a videotaped deposition in their notice of deposition. Similarly, the defending attorneys must decide whether to videotape a deposition where the examining attorney has decided only to record by stenographic means. This tactical decision involves weighing the advantages and disadvantages of videotaping as they relate specifically to each deponent.

The initial question which examining attorneys should ask is whether this deponent will be available at

DEPOSITIONS: Procedures, Strategy and Techniques, designed for use in CLE programs, is the textual abridgement of the looseleaf edition which includes forms on disk. The section and form numbering from the looseleaf edition have been retained in the Professional Education Edition.

trial. If the deponent will be available at trial, the fact-
finder will have the opportunity to observe the witness
even if the deposition has not been videotaped.

If the deponent might not be available at trial
because of serious illness or because the trial court's
subpoena power cannot compel attendance, then the
examining attorney should ask the following fundamental question: is it desirable to have the fact-finder see
and hear this deponent's testimony?

In answering that question, the examining attorney
should consider whether the witness is hostile or friendly. Friendly witnesses, including representatives of the
party, typically will come to trial. But, occasionally
attorneys can anticipate that a friendly witness will not
be available at trial. In that situation, the examining
attorney should consider whether the witness is "photogenic." Photogenic in this context means that the witness will appear credible when seen testifying. A friendly and photogenic witness who might not be available at
trial should be videotaped. That witness' deposition can
be used in evidence for any purpose. If, however, the
friendly witness is not photogenic, the examining attorney still should videotape that witness' deposition unless
the witness' poor appearance greatly outweighs the sig-
nificance of the witness' testimony. In other words, the
only friendly witnesses who should not be videotaped are
those who are both relatively insignificant and non-
photogenic.

Determining whether to videotape a hostile witness,
including representatives of the adversary, can be more
difficult. The deposition of an adverse party can be used
for any purpose. Presumably, the examining attorney
could conduct a videotaped deposition and then replay
designated portions of it as substantive evidence at trial.
The live testimony of the witness, however, is likely to
be more effective than even a videotaped deposition.
Alternatively, the witness could be called live at trial,
and the videotaped deposition could be used to impeach.
When the hostile deponent makes admissions or offers

DEPOSITIONS: Procedures, Strategy and Techniques, designed for use in CLE programs, is the textual
abridgement of the looseleaf edition which includes forms on disk. The section and form numbering
from the looseleaf edition have been retained in the Professional Education Edition.

deposition testimony that is ripe for use as impeachment, the well-orchestrated use of the videotape of that deposition testimony at trial can be extremely effective. Accordingly, even hostile witnesses who will be available at trial generally should be videotaped.

Despite the lack of familiarity which some attorneys have with videotaped depositions and despite the costs, attorneys' tactical interests generally are served by videotaping the deposition.

§ 5.4 The Mechanics of the Videotaped Deposition

The following step-by-step procedure is unique to a videotaped deposition:

1. *Serve proper notice*

After the examining attorney decides to videotape the deposition, that attorney must designate that the deposition will be videotaped in the notice of deposition. *See, e.g.,* Fed.R.Civ.P. 30(b).

2. *Make sure that an officer attends*

Unless stipulated otherwise, the deposition must be attended by an officer capable of administering oaths to the deponent. *See e.g.,* Fed.R.Civ.P. 30(b)(4).

3. *Select an operator*

Although the deposition must be attended by an officer, the officer need not be the video operator. Three types of video operators currently exist: attorneys, traditional court-reporters and production companies. Some attorneys have become excellent video operators in the course of using video throughout their practice. Conceivably, the examining attorney or a member of the examining attorney's firm or support staff can operate the video equipment during the deposition. Because lawyers or support staff are not qualified to be officers in the case, however, another person who is qualified to administer oaths must also be in attendance.

DEPOSITIONS: Procedures, Strategy and Techniques, designed for use in CLE programs, is the textual abridgement of the looseleaf edition which includes forms on disk. The section and form numbering from the looseleaf edition have been retained in the Professional Education Edition.

Many court-reporting agencies have branched into the field of video operations. Typically, these video operators are also qualified to be officers in the deposition and to administer oaths. They are intimately familiar with the deposition process. Attorneys (and judges) tend to feel comfortable with their presence in the deposition because it is familiar.

Alternatively, the examining attorney can find many video production teams or companies willing to take the deposition. These companies are professional. But they tend to be expensive and not familiar with the deposition process.

4. *Understand the equipment*

No matter who actually videotapes the deposition, the lawyer should have a working knowledge of the tools of the operation. The video camera, of course, is the key component in the system. Some operators will have two cameras, others will use only one pivotal camera. The camera or cameras together with the microphone pick up sound and light which is recorded in a VCR. Most equipment includes a date and time indicator on the tape itself so that attorneys quickly can locate the desired testimony.

From the point of view of the examining attorney, however, the most important piece of equipment may be the video monitor. Like a television, the monitor allows the examining attorney to check the deposition set-up and the nature of the images during the process itself. The examining attorney should make sure that the monitor is located at a place where it can be readily viewed by that attorney during the deposition. The examining attorney also should attempt to obtain from the operator a microphone that can be attached to the examiner's clothing. Such attachable microphones are preferable in convenience and sound quality to stand alone microphones. Finally, most video operators have devices—sometimes called mixers—which can segregate overlapping sounds and record each separately. Such a

---

DEPOSITIONS: Procedures, Strategy and Techniques, designed for use in CLE programs, is the textual abridgement of the looseleaf edition which includes forms on disk. The section and form numbering from the looseleaf edition have been retained in the Professional Education Edition.

device is invaluable in a deposition where attorneys and witnesses often talk at the same time.

5. *Position the camera*

The examining attorney should take charge of the deposition set-up, including the position of the camera relative to the deponent. The procedural rules generally require only that the appearance or the demeanor of the deponent not be distorted by recording techniques. *See, e.g.,* Fed.R.Civ.P. 30(b)(4). Without distorting the deponent, however, the examining attorney can use camera positioning to tactical advantage.

First, the examining attorney should have the camera operator film the deposition surroundings. The operator may capture the entirety of the room in which the examination is to take place. In addition, the operator may shift from person to person as they introduce themselves, or as the initial deposition formalities are observed.

After the setting is established, the camera should settle upon a position which captures the view of the deponent which most closely approximates the view which the jury would have of a live trial witness. Accordingly, the camera angle should be wide enough to catch the upper half of the deponent's body. The camera should not swing back and forth from the deponent to the examiner. Rather the camera should either fix upon the witness, or should fix upon both the examiner and the witness in the same shot. Where two cameras are used, the operator ultimately can employ split-screen or editing techniques to capture the examiner and the deponent at the same time or in succession.

As a general rule, the operator should not vary the camera angle and space after the basic position is established. An extreme close-up shot can distort the witness' appearance and highlight facial movements in an unduly prejudicial manner. Conversely, extreme long-range shots can suggest that the witness' testimony is insignificant. Where the examining attorney shows the

DEPOSITIONS: Procedures, Strategy and Techniques, designed for use in CLE programs, is the textual abridgement of the looseleaf edition which includes forms on disk. The section and form numbering from the looseleaf edition have been retained in the Professional Education Edition.

witness an exhibit, however, that attorney legitimately may "cue" the camera operator to get an extreme close-up of the exhibit.

6. *Control the process*

As with any deposition, the examining attorney must maintain control over the deposition process. In particular, the examiner should direct the witness and the camera or cameras to desired positions. The examiner should select the camera angle and the camera shots throughout the process. The examiner should orally "cue" the witness and the camera operator. The only voice in command of the deposition should be that of the examiner. Accordingly, the examiner should consult with the video operator before the deposition, so that the operator need not make a sound during the actual taping. To the extent that the operator needs to inform the examiner of mechanical issues such as poor positioning or limited time left on the tape, the operator should use nonverbal hand-signals.

Most court systems require officers to introduce themselves, the deposition and the persons present, and to administer the oath. *See e.g.* Fed.R.Civ.P. 30(b)(4). In a videotaped deposition, the officer may be required to make these introductory statements at the beginning of each tape. But, even these introductory statements can and should be "cued" by the examiner.

§ 5.5 Questioning Techniques Unique to Video-taped Examination

Attorneys should not alter their fundamental strategic objectives for a deposition merely because it will be videotaped. Attorneys should, however, take into consideration the fact that the deposition will be videotaped in organizing the deposition, forming the questions and interacting with the deponent. Videotape not only captures the full range of the deponent's oral and nonverbal communication, it also captures the full range of the examiner's oral and nonverbal communication. The examiner must remember that, unlike a stenographically

DEPOSITIONS: Procedures, Strategy and Techniques, designed for use in CLE programs, is the textual abridgement of the looseleaf edition which includes forms on disk. The section and form numbering from the looseleaf edition have been retained in the Professional Education Edition.

recorded deposition, the tone of voice used in the question will be captured. In a stenographically recorded deposition, attorneys frequently use tone of voice to elicit a designed response from the deponent. The transcript does not communicate that tone of voice. Thus, the question and answer, when used in court, appear objective. In the videotaped deposition, attorneys can still employ voice tone as a tactical weapon, but they must be aware that their tone of voice will not be concluded from the judge and the ultimate factfinder. Similarly, in the stenographic deposition attorneys often use facial gestures, posture and even head-nodding to draw out the deponent's responses. In videotaped depositions where the video camera captures the examiner, however, these nonverbal cues cannot be hidden. In other words, many of the tricks of the trade which have developed because depositions generally have been only transcribed in written form, will not be effective in a videotaped deposition. Indeed, they may be counterproductive to the extent that they communicate the examiner's efforts to trick the witness. Furthermore, the posturing, speech and arguing that consume so many stenographically recorded depositions should have no place in a videotaped deposition.

As a general guide, therefore, attorneys should treat a videotaped deposition examination as a dress rehearsal for trial. The examiners style and manner should be a courtroom style and manner. In fact, the examiner would do well to imagine that the factfinder is *present* in the deposition room. The examiner should conduct the examination in an organized and coherent fashion, adopting a tone appropriate to the witness' role in the trial. Because the deposition is not the trial, however, the examiner is free to attempt to discover new information. The examiner need not worry about pursuing lines of questioning that are unproductive. The deposition can and should be edited to remove a question or questioning which is extraneous, or which does not support the examiner's case.

DEPOSITIONS: Procedures, Strategy and Techniques, designed for use in CLE programs, is the textual abridgement of the looseleaf edition which includes forms on disk. The section and form numbering from the looseleaf edition have been retained in the Professional Education Edition.

§ 5.6 Defending Videotaped Depositions

Preparing a witness for a videotaped deposition presents unique challenges. First, the attorney must advise the deponent that all verbal and nonverbal cues will be recorded. Nonverbal cues include the appearance and clothing of the deponent. Deponents should wear formal, courtroom attire. They should wear solid colors. Plaid, herring bone tweeds and stripes tend to appear to vibrate on camera. Because bright and dark colors create glare, the witness should wear neutral blues or greys. Makeup, which becomes exaggerated on camera, should be used sparingly. On the other hand, the witness should be careful to remove any moisture from the skin. Men should shave immediately before the deposition.

Posture also communicates a message. The deponent should be instructed to maintain strong upright posture, unless the image of "victim" is desirable. Facial expressions are exaggerated on videotape. Accordingly, the defending attorney should instruct the deponent to attempt to maintain neutral facial expressions. Similarly, hand gestures, body movements and fidgeting are exaggerated on film. The deponent should be told to try to avoid these movements. The witness should maintain a relatively fixed position throughout the deposition.

Eye-contact conveys messages about the witness' credibility. The witness should maintain eye-contact with either the examiner or the camera. Such eye-contact conveys poise and security. When the witness looks down at the table or up at the ceiling after a question has been asked, that witness may appear to be insecure of the answer or even evasive. Because the witness should look the examiner in the eye, the witness may be more vulnerable to the examiner's nonverbal cues. Accordingly, the witness must be told to ignore those cues and to respond only to the question asked.

DEPOSITIONS: Procedures, Strategy and Techniques, designed for use in CLE programs, is the textual abridgement of the looseleaf edition which includes forms on disk. The section and form numbering from the looseleaf edition have been retained in the Professional Education Edition.

Videotape records the time lag between the question and the answer. When a camera is rolling, that dead time can seem interminable. The witness should take enough time to formulate proper answers to the question, but not so much time as to suggest uncertainty. If the defending attorney senses that the time-gap between question and answer is becoming problematic, that attorney may consider interposing an appropriate objection or asking the witness whether the question was comprehensible. At the same time, however, a defending attorney must never appear to be an obstructionist.

Because the videotape records the nature and extent of any conferences which the witness has with counsel during a deposition, such conferences should be kept to a minimum. If the witness appears to be nervous or to be having difficulty with a question or sense of questions, the examining attorney should simply take a break. Frequent breaks may be the only way for a defending attorney to control a particularly tense videotaped deposition.

If the defending attorney devotes sufficient time and resources to the preparation of the deponent for a videotaped deposition, such tactics should be unnecessary. Videotape presents preparation issues different from stenographic recording. Each of those issues can be addressed with the deponent. Yet, the only way to insure that deponents (and their counsel) are fully prepared for a videotaped deposition is to rehearse. At least a part of the preparation session with the deponent should be a videotaped rehearsal of the deposition itself. After the videotape rehearsal is completed, the defending attorney and the deponent should review the videotape together with a keen eye toward nonverbal communication issues such as appearance, clothing, posture, gestures, eye-contact and poise in responding to difficult questions. After this session, the attorney should videotape additional rehearsal sessions until both the attorney and the deponent feel comfortable with the form and the substance of the deponent's responses.

DEPOSITIONS: Procedures, Strategy and Techniques, designed for use in CLE programs, is the textual abridgement of the looseleaf edition which includes forms on disk. The section and form numbering from the looseleaf edition have been retained in the Professional Education Edition.

Chapter 6

PRE–DEPOSITION PROCEDURES

Table of Sections

---

§ 6.5 Putting Nonverbal Cues on the Record

Whether the examiner wishes to put on the record the deponent's conduct will be a strategic decision made at the time. Where a deponent is intentionally evasive or hostile, placing such cues on the record may be strategically important to letting the deponent know these tactics do not go unnoticed. More effectively, however, a deponent who is seemingly evasive or unresponsive out of nervousness or uncertainty should be encouraged to relax and reminded that so long as the truth is told, the deponent should be confident and comfortable. In the latter case, the intimidation created by making a record is avoided in favor of a supportive measure.

§ 6.6 Assisting the Court Reporter

The examiner must recognize the important role played by the court reporter. The reporter records all testimony and objections which occur during the deposition. In order to reduce the possibility of transcript errors during the deposition, the reporter should be made as comfortable as possible. The examiner can assist the reporter by providing prior to the deposition a

---

DEPOSITIONS: Procedures, Strategy and Techniques, designed for use in CLE programs, is the textual abridgement of the looseleaf edition which includes forms on disk. The section and form numbering from the looseleaf edition have been retained in the Professional Education Edition.

caption of the case, spellings of difficult names or terms to be used during the deposition and a copy of anything likely to be read into the record. Breaks should be taken every 60 to 90 minutes not only to permit the deponent and participants to relax and re-gather thoughts, but also to allow the court reporter to rejuvenate his or her own energies. *See* Form 6–1.

Maintaining a proper professional relationship with the court reporter can result in a more complete transcript. Excellent reporters will, on their own initiative, "clean up the transcript" by eliminating false starts of the attorney or non-question cluttering such as "I see", "o.k." or repetition of responses. If an attorney wishes these types of phrases to appear on the record, they should request the court reporter to transcribe the interaction verbatim without any editorial clean-up. Court reporters are, of course, human and will tend to assist those attorneys who treat them well. For example, deponents who give a nonverbal response such as "uh huh" may be requested by the court reporter to state a verbal response, if the examiner forgets to do so. Other reporters will do nothing unless specifically requested by an attorney. Antagonizing the reporter will discourage him or her from providing such procedural assistance. As officers of the court, the reporter has the obligation to ensure an accurate and complete transcription of the interaction, but responsibilities get exercised differently by different reporters; their view of their own role will vary as well. As a result, attorneys are best advised to maintain good relations with the court reporter.

§ 6.7 Agreeing to "the Usual Stipulations"

It is not uncommon after the introductory amenities, for a court reporter or the presenting attorney to ask whether all parties present will agree to "the usual stipulations." Some attorneys readily agree to these stipulations; most attorneys do not know what these stipulations are to which they have just agreed. The

DEPOSITIONS: Procedures, Strategy and Techniques, designed for use in CLE programs, is the textual abridgement of the looseleaf edition which includes forms on disk. The section and form numbering from the looseleaf edition have been retained in the Professional Education Edition.

examiner should request that any stipulation be speci-fied onto the record.

Following is a list of potential stipulations:

(1) Agreement that the deposition will be taken pursuant to "Rules of Civil Procedure." This stipula-tion is superfluous because all applicable civil procedural and court rules govern the interaction whether or not the attorneys agree that they do so. Attorneys may not agree to waive any governing deposition rules. Thus, there is little purpose in making the stipulation.

(2) Agreement to waive the oath. There is purpose in an attempt to waive the oath. Whether the deposi-tion is used as an impeachment tool at trial or is to be read into evidence at trial, it is imperative that the testimony be given under oath. It would be catastrophic for the deponent to be asked at trial: "and you were sworn to tell the truth at the deposition, weren't you?" with the answer: "no, I recall the attorneys agreeing to waive the oath, so I was not sworn." The examining attorney must ensure that all deponents explicitly take an oath on the record.

(3) Agree to waive the reading and signing of the deposition transcript. Federal Rule 30(e) and its state analogues require the deponent or a party to request review and signature of the transcript during the deposi-tion itself. The absence of a formal request constitutes a waiver. This request should always be made. The reporter's duties are difficult and often tedious; the likelihood of error at some point is always present. Attorneys should expend the time it takes to read and ensure the accuracy of the deposition transcript. The parties may, however, agree that the transcript be signed before any notary. This agreement is useful when the deponent lives at a great distance from the deposition site and it would be inconvenient for that person to sign the transcript in the presence of a partic-ular court reporter. *See* Blumenkopf, Deposition Strate-gy and Tactics, 5 Am.J.Tr.Adv. 231, 239 (1981).

There is a strategic reason for providing the deponent with the opportunity to read and sign the transcript. Where the deponent has the opportunity, but makes no such changes, the strength of impeachment is enhanced for trial. The mechanism relies on the fact that Federal Rule of Civil Procedure 30(e) extends the right to require the reading and signing to "any party." Many lawyers tend to believe that the right belongs only to the deponent or to the deponent's lawyer, but it in fact belongs to any party.

Therefore, the lawyer who requires the review has the potential for a nice moment at trial when he or she wishes to confront and impeach the witness. "You recall giving your deposition on June 19th? And you recall being given the opportunity to read the transcript and make any changes that you wished to make, isn't that correct? In fact, *I* am the one who gave you that right by requesting that you read and sign the transcript, isn't that right?"

The only risk taken is that the deponent will actually read and change the transcript. In most cases, the risk is low because many deponents tend to let the time pass which leads to the transcript being considered correct automatically after 30 days. (see FRCP 30). Where the deponent does make a change, the chance is still low that he or she will change the particular answer you seek to challenge. Nevertheless, there is a risk and the lawyer must make a fair calculation.

(4) Agree that withdrawn questions will be omitted from the transcript. This stipulation creates a cleaner record, and saves transcription costs. In addition, it benefits the examining attorney because any unpreparedness, confusion, or strategy inherent in such comments gets eliminated from the transcript.

(5) Agreement that all evidentiary objections will be preserved until trial. Such an agreement may be invalid under Fed.R.Civ.P. 32 since the Rule requires that "errors and irregularities occurring at the oral examination

DEPOSITIONS: Procedures, Strategy and Techniques, designed for use in CLE programs, is the textual abridgement of the looseleaf edition which includes forms on disk. The section and form numbering from the looseleaf edition have been retained in the Professional Education Edition.

... in the form of the question ... are waived unless seasonable objection thereto is made at the taking of the deposition.'' The Rule's language is mandatory; any stipulation to the contrary could be deemed invalid at trial. In that circumstance, the failure to object to the form of a question at deposition will constitute a waiver of the objection at trial.

(6) Agreement that any opposing attorney's objection inures to the benefit of all. This stipulation precludes other attorneys from having to make the same objection on the record. The stipulation results in fewer and shorter interruptions, thereby benefiting the examining attorney.

(7) Agreement that an instruction from counsel that the deponent not answer shall be deemed the equivalent of the deponent's refusal to answer. Such a stipulation saves time by eliminating the necessary steps to certifying the question. However, where a deponent seems independent or does not otherwise act in conjunction with his attorney, such a stipulation should be strategically avoided as many answers may likely be gained in the face of contrary advice from the defending attorney.

§ 6.8 The Procedural Rules

The examiner routinely begins the deposition by stating a series of rules which establish a framework for the interaction. These rules keep the court reporter's record clear and establish proper decorum during the deposition. Most examining attorneys state some or all of these rules in a drone or matter-of-fact tone of voice. By so doing, the examiner gives up an important opportunity to establish his or her own credibility for the deponent. Rather, the attorney should state each of the following rules in question form to ensure the deponent's understanding and adherence to each of them. Explicit understanding established on the record will be useful should the transcript need to be used to impeach during trial.

DEPOSITIONS: Procedures, Strategy and Techniques, designed for use in CLE programs, is the textual abridgement of the looseleaf edition which includes forms on disk. The section and form numbering from the looseleaf edition have been retained in the Professional Education Edition.

Some defending attorneys will interrupt the reading of the rules by noting that they properly prepared the deponent and informed him of the rules. When confronted with this tactic, the examiner should persist in stating the rules to both maintain control of the deposition and establish, on the record, the deponent's understanding of the following rules:

(1) I'm going to ask you a series of questions regarding the incident that is the subject of this lawsuit and which occurred on _____. Do you understand this?

(2) If at any time you don't understand one of my questions, please say so and I will repeat or rephrase it until you do understand the question. Do you understand this rule?

(3) If at any time you don't hear one of my questions, please say so and I will repeat it to ensure that you do hear it. Do you understand?

(4) All of your answers must be verbal since the court reporter cannot take down non-verbal cues such as a nod of the head or shrug of the shoulders. Do you understand that all your responses must be stated in words? [Many deponents will answer this question with an "uh huh" which should then be followed by clarifying that they have just violated the rule.]

(5) If you do not know the answer to a question, simply state you do not know. I do not expect you to guess or to speculate as to responses. Do you understand?

(6) Please make your answers clear for the record so the court reporter can accurately transcribe each of the words you state. Do you understand this?

(7) Please wait until I finish each of my questions before answering and I will wait until you finish each of your answers before I ask another question. In this way the court reporter keeps a clear record without interruption. Do you understand?

DEPOSITIONS: Procedures, Strategy and Techniques, designed for use in CLE programs, is the textual abridgement of the looseleaf edition which includes forms on disk. The section and form numbering from the looseleaf edition have been retained in the Professional Education Edition.

(8) We will take a break about every hour to give the court reporter and all of us a chance to refresh ourselves. If you need a break prior to that time, please request one and we will take one. Do you understand?

(9) You understand that the deposition will be transcribed by the court reporter and that everything said here today will be recorded. Do you understand that?

(10) You understand that, at trial, all the testimony given here today will be available in written form, and if I ask you a question at trial that I ask you today, you may be asked to explain or otherwise account for any difference in your answers that may occur. Do you understand?

(11) You understand that your testimony today is being given under oath, as if you were in a court of law, *i.e.*, you have been sworn to tell the truth and if you fail to do so adverse consequences could result. Do you understand?

(12) And finally, the deponent must be asked the catch-all question: Do you understand each and every one of these rules as I have stated them? If the deponent answers in the negative, the examiner must take the time to uncover which rule was unclear and review that rule with the deponent. If the deponent answers in the affirmative, the examiner should follow up with this final statement: "That's fine. You understand that these rules assure that if I ask a question and you give an answer to that question it will be assumed that you understood the question as posed and your answer is intended to be responsive as rendered. Do you understand this statement?" This final affirmation fairly precludes any claim at trial by the deponent that a question was confusing or an answer was not responsive due to a poorly phrased question.

The recitation of these rules establishes both attorney tone and control. If a cordial relationship is desired, these initial remarks should be stated in a friendly manner. A more stern, formal atmosphere necessitates

DEPOSITIONS: Procedures, Strategy and Techniques, designed for use in CLE programs, is the textual abridgement of the looseleaf edition which includes forms on disk. The section and form numbering from the looseleaf edition have been retained in the Professional Education Edition.

a more rigid recitation of the rules. Deponents respond to the atmosphere created by the examiner during these initial moments. Thus, the rules are an integral part of an effective deposition, and should be stated with meaning.

§ 6.9 Use of Exhibits

Whenever possible, the examining attorney should have exhibits organized and marked for use prior to the deposition. *See* Form 6–2. The ritual of having the court reporter mark the deposition during the interaction, though archaic, is generally employed. An attorney can mark each exhibit with the name of the deponent, date of the deposition and number of the exhibit (ordered in some sequential fashion) as part of effective planning. Exhibits are marked to keep the record clear. The attorney should remember that statements such as "Let the record reflect the deponent has marked the photograph" leave ambiguity as to which photograph, what was marked, and where the photograph was marked. All markings made on an exhibit or reference made to the exhibit should be made clearly, leaving no ambiguity on the record. Attaching to the deposition transcript a copy of each exhibit eliminates potential confusion over which exhibit was used in the deposition. Certainly the record will be confused if an exhibit is not described in a fashion which distinguishes it from other exhibits.

Whether marked before or during the deposition, the examiner should describe the exhibit at least once on the record. For example:

ATTORNEY: Court reporter, kindly mark as Mr. Jones' Exhibit No. 1 this three inch by five inch photograph, depicting the front of the post office and date stamped July 29, 1988.

The examiner, out of professional courtesy, should show the exhibit to opposing counsel so that all attorneys are knowledgeable of the exhibit being discussed.

DEPOSITIONS: Procedures, Strategy and Techniques, designed for use in CLE programs, is the textual abridgement of the looseleaf edition which includes forms on disk. The section and form numbering from the looseleaf edition have been retained in the Professional Education Edition.

Introducing an exhibit in a deposition is not fraught with the technicalities of "offering" that exhibit into evidence at trial. At deposition, the exhibit automatically becomes part of the record; objections are for trial. There is also no need to lay a foundation for questioning a deponent about an exhibit, unless the deposition is to be read into evidence at trial for an unavailable witness; thus, establishing foundation can prevent subsequent admission problems at a trial.

Be certain to avoid the "this and that" problem. This occurs when lawyers referencing exhibits on the record forget that the record must be kept clear. As a result, they will conduct an examination as follows:

"Now you have seen this? And then you were shown that one? Now which of these were definitive to your decision?" The responses to these questions will be meaningless and worth little as a tool of impeachment. A "yes" or "no" will not clarify anything. What is "this?" What is "that one?" There is no way to make this clear for a jury when and if the time comes.

The answer is to be specific. "Now you have seen what is marked Exhibit 2? And then you were shown this photo, which is Exhibit 7? Now which of these were definitive to your decision, Exhibit 2 or 7?" If the deponent responds, "that one," be certain to clarify the response on the record, "that would be Exhibit 7?" Seemingly common sense and simple, when in the middle of an exchange, it is more than easy to forget the importance of keeping the record clear.

*

Form 6-2

Organization of Exhibits

Case _____   File No. _____

Date of Deposition _____   Deponent _____

Issue: _____

Question	Document Needed-Title	Cite	Exhibit No.

Issue: _____

Question	Document Needed-Title	Cite	Exhibit No.

Issue: _____

Question	Document Needed-Title	Cite	Exhibit No.

Form 6-2
[G20,514]

*

Part II

THE DEPOSING ATTORNEY'S PERSPECTIVE

•

Chapter 7

EFFECTIVE DEPOSITION QUESTIONING

Table of Sections

---

§ 7.1   Understanding How Deponents Think

If we could step into the deponent's mind, we would be better able to determine and evaluate the manner in

---

DEPOSITIONS: Procedures, Strategy and Techniques, designed for use in CLE programs, is the textual abridgement of the looseleaf edition which includes forms on disk. The section and form numbering from the looseleaf edition have been retained in the Professional Education Edition.

which that person thinks and processes information. Knowing this, the deposing lawyer can formulate questions that better align with the reality of each juror. Understanding this process produces powerful potential for adjusting questions so they are better able to elicit information from the deponent.

The process of communication, and the science of neurolinguistic programming (NLP) rely primarily on three of our five human senses: sight (visual), sound (auditory), and touch or feeling (kinesthetic). Each of us uses each of the three processing modes at various times, but carries a preference for one of them. The deposing lawyer's goal is to identify the means by which the deponent prefers to process information and then modify inquiries accordingly. Paul M. Lisnek, "Finding Jurors with Open Minds Requires Looking Inside," *Chicago Daily Law Bulletin,* March 15, 1993, p. 6; Paul M. Lisnek and Eric Oliver, *The Complete Litigator,* Andrews Professional Books (Westtown, PA, 1994).

Many deponents will be primarily visual processors. Their minds work like a view master, transforming input into pictures for interpretation. For example, when visual based people describe events in which they were involved, they will describe those events by describing the pictures which fly through their minds. *Id.* Your deposition questions should guide that juror towards retrieving visual information. For example, "what did that look like to you?" or, "how did you come to see that document?" These inquiries feed into the visual processor's mind and are more likely to elicit a response than auditory or feeling based inquiries.

Other people prefer naturally to think and process information in words or sounds. These auditory based people have a constant discussion going on in their head; they react primarily to the sounds or voices that occupy their mind. They listen to and for details and can locate the logical connections between ideas; asked to envision a scene or feel emotion these deponents respond with difficulty. Your questions should guide them to process

DEPOSITIONS: Procedures, Strategy and Techniques, designed for use in CLE programs, is the textual abridgement of the looseleaf edition which includes forms on disk. The section and form numbering from the looseleaf edition have been retained in the Professional Education Edition.

auditory information. "How would you say you came across this document?" or, "Tell me what you did first." These inquiries feed into the processing mode of the auditory person.

People who think in terms of feelings operate on an emotional level, rather than responding to what they see or hear. They rely on gut reactions and feelings. People who think this way convert external information into a feeling, then sense the feeling, and finally transform their feelings into terms they can communicate. For example, "what sense do you have of how close the other car was to yours?" or "does it seem right to you that this document was forwarded on without your review?"

People provide "clues" as to how they are thinking at any given point in time; deposing lawyers need to learn how to tap into them. *id.* These indicators include posture, gestures, breathing and many others. The easiest of all the indicators to describe are the words selected by the deponent and the way in which they move their eyes. Visually oriented people will use visual words including: clear, picture, focus, see, foggy. They will use phrases such as "I see what you mean; Picture this for a moment; In my view; Imagine if you will; Crystal clear; Don't look so blue in the face; He has a dark personality; He appears so transparent." When asked a question, a visual deponent will flick the eyes up and to the right or left to find the answer. While eye movement may not be exaggerated, a subtle shift of the eye in the upwards direction indicates a search for a visual answer. For right-handed persons, looking up and to their right means that they are creating or constructing a visual image. If they look up and to their left, they are remembering a visual image. Periodically, persons will create visual images by staring straight ahead and dramatically de-focusing their eyes. (the eye movement of a left-handed person is opposite regarding creating and remembering information, respectively). *id.*

DEPOSITIONS: Procedures, Strategy and Techniques, designed for use in CLE programs, is the textual abridgement of the looseleaf edition which includes forms on disk. The section and form numbering from the looseleaf edition have been retained in the Professional Education Edition.

Auditory-based deponents will select sound-based words to describe what is happening in their mind. They select words like: sound, hear, listen, say, talk and rings. They will therefore use phrases such as, "I hear what you mean; That sounds good to me; That rings a bell; Talk to me for a minute; I want you to explain ...; That clicks for me; Everyone is clamoring for my attention." Auditory-based eye movements are side to side. Right-handed persons looking to their right are indicating that they are constructing or creating a sound. Looking to their left, means they are remembering a sound. The opposite is true for left-handed persons. *id.*

The feeling-based person selects tactile words that include: comfort, feel, grasp, or handle. They will use phrases such as "I'm uncomfortable with ...; I want to grasp this situation; There's a hot idea; I just don't feel that ...; That kind of talk is hard to handle." Kinesthetic-based persons look down and to their left (opposite for the left-handed person) to access feelings. These downward glances are often subtle. For example, deponents asked how they feel about something, will look up to visualize the situation, and then downward to get in touch with the feelings related to the mental picture created.

Keep notes on the words, phrases and eye movements of deponents during the first several response to deposition questions. Questions should be structured to permit the deponent to process in the way most comfortable for him or her. Ask a visual deponent to "describe" experiences, an auditory deponent to "tell you about" and a feeling deponent for "her sense of ...," Observe eye movement as you ask for known factual information (address and family situation) to test for consistency. Once a sense is gathered about that deponent, you can explore relevant attitudes and observe to see how they access and report information. *id.* Imagine the power of controlling questioning at this level.

Lawyers who understand information processing will create better deposition questions, those which align

DEPOSITIONS: Procedures, Strategy and Techniques, designed for use in CLE programs, is the textual abridgement of the looseleaf edition which includes forms on disk. The section and form numbering from the looseleaf edition have been retained in the Professional Education Edition.

with the deponent's preferred processing mode. The result is control over the deposition interaction. For a complete discussion of information processing, see Paul M. Lisnek, *Effective Client Communication: A Lawyer's Handbook to Interviewing and Counseling,* West Publishing Company, St. Paul, MN, 1992, Chapter 2; Paul M. Lisnek and Eric Oliver, *The Complete Litigator,* Andrews Professional Books (Westtown, PA, 1994).

§ 7.2 Availability of Leading Questions

Most deponents are warned by their attorneys not to volunteer information or otherwise assist the examiner in the deposition. The examiner must therefore be prepared to elicit information strategically and carefully. There are a series of questioning techniques available to examiners; selecting the desirable technique will depend upon the phase of the deposition.

Deposing a person aligned with the opposition permits the examiner the right to lead, or create the flavor of a cross-examination. Whenever a party deposes a hostile witness, an adverse party or a witness identified with an adverse party, the interrogation may proceed by leading questions in accordance with Fed.R.Ev. 611(c). While the examiner has the right to lead, he may choose not to do so depending on the purpose of his question or the area of inquiry. For example, when the examiner's central purpose is to gather information, the use of leading questions will be limited. Conversely, when the examiner wishes to pin down certain testimony, leading questions provide the same control as cross-examination at trial. The fundamental rule that a deposition may operate like a cross examination is one not often remembered or employed by most examining attorneys. In fact, many examiners retreat from an objection by opposing counsel to the use of leading questions. Examiners simply need to remember their right to use leading questions during depositions. The type of question used will vary with the phase of the deposition.

DEPOSITIONS: Procedures, Strategy and Techniques, designed for use in CLE programs, is the textual abridgement of the looseleaf edition which includes forms on disk. The section and form numbering from the looseleaf edition have been retained in the Professional Education Edition.

§ 7.3 Areas of Inquiry

The examiner typically inquires into three areas: the background of the deponent, the cause of action and the injury or damages (past, present and future) incurred. This outline represents the usual order in which questioning is conducted, but no rule precludes an examining attorney from modifying the order or beginning at any desired point. In fact, beginning a deposition at a key or crucial fact-issue can take the other participants off guard thereby preventing them from responding with a carefully designed answer created prior to the deposition. The examiner's central objective is to exhaust the witness's knowledge about the facts in the case. For this reason, a checklist approach to depositions is not recommended. There are a variety of checklist sources on the market, but the attorney who scripts the interaction risks the loss of effective follow-up and probing which follows in the interaction, not on a checklist. Form 7–1 provides an alternative and rather unique means of preparing for questioning. By creating a question tree, the attorney uses logic and follow-up to pursue each potential answer given by a deponent. The deposition retains flexibility but also issues completeness as each branch of the question tree, for any particular issue, is followed up.

Examples of how Form 7–1 can be completed follow on the next pages.

DEPOSITIONS: Procedures, Strategy and Techniques, designed for use in CLE programs, is the textual abridgement of the looseleaf edition which includes forms on disk. The section and form numbering from the looseleaf edition have been retained in the Professional Education Edition.

Question Tree – Background

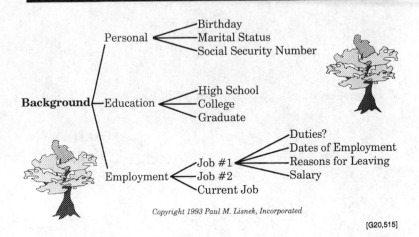

Background
- Personal
  - Birthday
  - Marital Status
  - Social Security Number
- Education
  - High School
  - College
  - Graduate
- Employment
  - Job #1
    - Duties?
    - Dates of Employment
    - Reasons for Leaving
    - Salary
  - Job #2
  - Current Job

Copyright 1993 Paul M. Lisnek, Incorporated

[G20,515]

Question Tree – Events

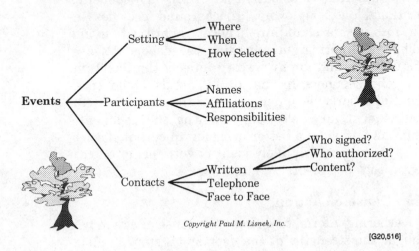

Events
- Setting
  - Where
  - When
  - How Selected
- Participants
  - Names
  - Affiliations
  - Responsibilities
- Contacts
  - Written
    - Who signed?
    - Who authorized?
    - Content?
  - Telephone
  - Face to Face

Copyright Paul M. Lisnek, Inc.

[G20,516]

Question Tree – Consequences

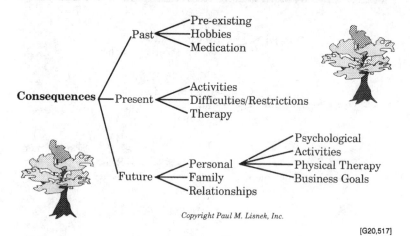

Past
- Pre-existing
- Hobbies
- Medication

Consequences

Present
- Activities
- Difficulties/Restrictions
- Therapy

Future
- Personal
  - Psychological
  - Activities
  - Physical Therapy
  - Business Goals
- Family
- Relationships

Copyright Paul M. Lisnek, Inc.

[G20,517]

§ 7.4 Background of Deponent

It is important to understand the deponent's general background and personal history. Understanding where the deponent currently lives and has lived provides information on his attitudes and desires as well as essential contact information. The attorney may wish to speak to neighbors or housemates regarding the deponent. Gathering information regarding a deponent's educational and employment background provides insight into his level of intelligence, sophistication and credibility. Information regarding the deponent's age, marital status and family history reflects the likely image of the deponent in the jurors' minds. The background of a party deponent provides information useful in subsequent jury selection; knowing the deponent's background provides a better basis for an educated selection of jurors who will likely identify with, or not identify with, that deponent.

§ 7.5 Cause of Action

Gathering information about the cause of action will highlight the strengths of the deponent's story and signal necessary defenses. The manner of questioning will depend on the approach chosen by the examiner, but the ultimate facts which reflect the legal issues must be investigated thoroughly. *See* Form 7–1. For example, the components in a tort case include proximate cause, standard of care, and breach of duty, each of which must be an area of inquiry. In addition, all of the complementary or evidentiary facts which may prove or disprove each of the ultimate facts must be investigated. Facts which weaken the deponent's position must be gathered to reduce the credibility of the deponent or the weight of the testimony in the event of trial or to posture for settlement.

§ 7.6 Damages

Damages or injuries represent a separate and major area of inquiry. Investigating all past, present and future damages is essential regardless of the position taken with regard to liability in the case. Moreover, the extent of damages impacts the value of potential settlement and helps determine verdict exposure.

§ 7.7 Question Format—Open vs. Closed Questions

The examiner should decide to use general, open-ended questions which elicit narrative answers, close-ended questions that clarify and probe, or a combination of both. As a rule, the examiner should begin with general inquiries and then shift to specific probes. It is easier for a deponent to first explain generalities, and then to clarify specifics.

So long as the examiner proceeds logically, he may shift the subject matter of the questions frequently and suddenly. This tactic limits the deponent's ability to give a planned answer when such a question is asked out of anticipated sequence. The use of open-ended questions permits the deponent to narrate answers freely and are quite useful unless the deponent rambles. The examiner structures responses by explaining or instructing the deponent to answer open-ended questions such

DEPOSITIONS: Procedures, Strategy and Techniques, designed for use in CLE programs, is the textual abridgement of the looseleaf edition which includes forms on disk. The section and form numbering from the looseleaf edition have been retained in the Professional Education Edition.

as "tell me everything that you said to him and he said to you in that conversation."

§ 7.8 Impeachment Information

The examiner may possess certain impeaching facts which he may wish to consider raising in the deposition. The examiner may wish to save the impeaching ammunition for trial, or disclose the information to intimidate an evasive witness into giving more truthful and complete answers. Raising impeaching information often leads a deponent to believe that the examiner knows more about the case than he admits, leading the deponent to be honest. Raising impeachment information can also motivate the deponent and other attorneys to settle the litigation.

§ 7.9 Estimating Distance and Time

Deponents are often hesitant to estimate distance and time. The examiner can deal with this issue in one of two ways:

1. If the examiner seeks information regarding distance and the deponent states that he is poor at estimating distance, the examiner may begin with extremely high estimates and ask the deponent in sequence whether the distance was greater or less than the exaggerated estimate. This technique locks the deponent into an estimate range.

2. The examiner may ask the deponent to specify the terms in which he would feel comfortable establishing an estimation. For example, some deponents cannot speak in feet but prefer to talk in terms of yards or car lengths. While estimating time or distance is a difficult concept, in general, the examiner can uncover a means by which the deponent will be able to render an estimate, at least in his own terms.

Consider the additional control provided by asking for distance and time with questions designed with the deponent's information processing preferences in mind.

DEPOSITIONS: Procedures, Strategy and Techniques, designed for use in CLE programs, is the textual abridgement of the looseleaf edition which includes forms on disk. The section and form numbering from the looseleaf edition have been retained in the Professional Education Edition.

See section 7.1. For example, standing at a certain distance from the deponent and asking, "is this about the right distance that car was from you when you first saw it?" Feeling based deponents can sense the proper answer and have the lawyer move until the proper distance is arrived at. Then, the lawyer must be certain to clarify the response for the record, "let the record reflect that I am at 6 feet from the deponent." The deposing lawyer should not be surprised when a feeling-based deponent can state, not only how far one car was from the other, but the type of car it was! Visual deponents may also be able to do this, but auditory people are far less likely to be able to relate such information. This latter information processor may need to tie into a remembered sound cue to establish distance.

§ 7.10 Closing Questions

The use of closing questions is important to specify the who, what, when, where, why and how questions. It is these components that produce detailed information necessary to complete each component of the deponent's story. Closing questions can clamp off an area: "Have you told us absolutely everything that you remember happening at that time?" or: "Do you remember anything else at all in response to this question?" The examiner should get all details of any conversations held with the deponent including exact quotations or, at a minimum, paraphrases of the conversation.

§ 7.13 The Importance of Follow–Up Questions

Although the interaction rules specify that deponents should request clarification of an unclear question, the effective examiner will nevertheless monitor himself to ensure that his questions are simple and clear. *See* Form 7–2. It makes sense to subdivide a question to better obtain an answer which is responsive. For example, an attorney who asks "You saw the witness and approached her?" Answer: "Yes." The record will be

---

DEPOSITIONS: Procedures, Strategy and Techniques, designed for use in CLE programs, is the textual abridgement of the looseleaf edition which includes forms on disk. The section and form numbering from the looseleaf edition have been retained in the Professional Education Edition.

ambiguous as to whether the deponent both first saw the witness *and* approached her, or that the deponent approached the witness, *or* was first to see the witness. The examiner must probe, follow-up, and maintain an inquisitive attitude throughout the deposition. As a rule, the deposition is the time to uncover any and all information, whether or not it proves to be damaging.

Where information is uncovered which may be damaging, the examiner is best advised not to react visibly, but to maintain a neutral "poker face." While case position may be shattered or unexpected follow-up work necessary, it is best for case posture for the examiner not to reveal surprise or dismay. After all, any and all facts are likely to be brought out in trial testimony. Always follow-up each fact uncovered by asking: "how do you know?" Where a witness specifies they do not know the answer to a question, always inquire: "who would know?" Such follow-up permits future depositions to be scheduled to obtain the necessary information.

§ 7.14 Deponent Answers—Generally

The examiner must monitor and control the witness and his responses to ensure accuracy and completeness. *See* Form 7–3.

§ 7.15 Unresponsive Answer

Where an answer is unresponsive, the examiner should insist that the witness restate the answer until it is complete and accurate. This may result in the deponent changing his answer to "I don't know," which may have been the truth in the first place. Oftentimes, a deponent's response is off the mark because he resorts to speculation. The follow-up ensures whether that deponent knows something first-hand which would respond directly to the question.

§ 7.16 Rambling Answer

When the deponent rambles, the examiner may either move to strike that portion of the answer which is

---

DEPOSITIONS: Procedures, Strategy and Techniques, designed for use in CLE programs, is the textual abridgement of the looseleaf edition which includes forms on disk. The section and form numbering from the looseleaf edition have been retained in the Professional Education Edition.

120

unresponsive or inform the deponent that he has answered the question. Where the deponent's testimony rambles but is favorable, the record nevertheless needs to be clarified: the examiner can restate and summarize the favorable testimony on the record and then confirm with the deponent that the summary is accurate.

§ 7.17 Incomplete Answer

Where the answer is incomplete, insist that the deponent give a complete and sufficient answer. Ask the deponent whether he knows anything else or inquire whether the deponent has stated everything he knows in full response to the question.

§ 7.18 Handling Objections Made as Strategy

Every non-examining attorney has a right to make an objection during the deposition. The examiner, however, also has the right to insist on an answer to the question, subject to the objection. Fed.R.Civ.P. 30(c). The only time that a witness may be instructed not to answer a question is when that instruction is necessary to preserve a privilege, to enforce an evidentiary limitation ordered by the court, or to present a motion to limit or terminate the examination due to the examiner's bad faith efforts to annoy, embarrass or oppress the deponent. Fed.R.Civ.P. 30(d)(1). As a practical matter, the examiner has the right to receive a complete answer to every question unless the question invades a legitimate privilege.

The examiner should monitor whether objections begin to interfere with the direction and goals of the deposition. Where an objecting attorney fails to specify grounds for the objection, and the examiner is uncertain of its basis, a request for explanation should be made on the record. An objection to a poorly phrased question gives the examiner an option to rephrase, withdraw or repeat the question. Often, an objection to relevance can be cured through rephrasing or asking other questions which establish a foundation. Even if the examin-

---

DEPOSITIONS: Procedures, Strategy and Techniques, designed for use in CLE programs, is the textual abridgement of the looseleaf edition which includes forms on disk. The section and form numbering from the looseleaf edition have been retained in the Professional Education Edition.

er chooses not to modify the question, he is nevertheless entitled to an answer to the question. Fed.R.Civ.P. 30(c). Objections based on any other ground may be "ignored" by the examiner who continues his request for a response from the deponent. Where the deponent appears unsure of how to proceed, the examiner should request the deponent to respond to the question, with the objection being handled by the lawyers at a later date.

Where the defending attorney instructs the deponent not to answer the question, the examiner should request the deponent to state his refusal to answer on the record (except where there has been a stipulation on this issue). The question should be certified on the record, which preserves the option of having the judge compel an answer. The transcript must clearly reflect the question not answered, the objection, and the instruction not to answer. Insufficient reasons for the objection may produce sanctions pursuant to Fed. R.Civ.P. 37, including costs rendered against the objecting attorney.

Where an attorney constantly imposes objections, he may do so as strategic interference with the interaction. The examiner may cooperatively remind the objector that most substantive objections are preserved for trial, there being no need to continue rendering objections. If a situation gets intolerable, the examiner may terminate the deposition to obtain a protective order or Fed. R.Civ.P. 37 sanction. *See* Fed.R.Civ.P. 30(d)(1).

The examiner must maintain control of the deposition. Where attorneys interfere with the direction of the deposition, the examiner must insist that the deposition proceed in his selected manner and direction. Where hostile discussions ensue, the examiner is best advised to keep all discussion on the record, including offensive non-verbal conduct. For example, specifying on the record that the defending attorney "need not pound your fist on the table and scream at a high pitch" records for a judge the requisite conduct to render sanctions against the offending attorney. A request for a recess may calm the participants, but may, like the objection, disrupt an excellent flow of an examiner's questions. Essentially, the examiner should monitor whether interferences are being made on a legitimate basis, or simply to interrupt the "effective roll" of the examiner; in the latter instance, the examiner is best advised to proceed after warning all other participants to respect the proper decorum of the proceedings.

§ 7.19 Requests for Recess

The defending attorney has the right to confer with his deponent during the questioning or during recess. Where the defending attorney passes the deponent a note for a conference, such conduct should be placed on the record by the examiner. Courts recognize the attorney's right to initiate a private conference for the purpose of determining whether a privilege should be asserted (*see* Standing Order 13 on Effective Discovery in Civil Cases, 102 F.R.D. 351 (E.D.N.Y.)), but some attorneys abuse this procedure by using private conferences to coach the deponent on responses.

Where a conference between a non-party deponent and an attorney occurs during a recess, the examiner should question the non-party deponent about the substance of the conference (as such is not protected by any privilege). Where the deponent is a party, the fact that a conversation occurred is not privileged even though the contents may be. The examiner can ask the deponent whether he wishes to change any testimony given before the recess as a result of his conference. Clearly, a changed response will likely appear at trial as the product of attorney prompting during the recess conference.

§ 7.20 Concluding the Deposition

The conclusion of a deposition often is as ritualistic as the opening. The examiner should solidify the testimony given by the deponent and specify any future commitments from that deponent. Verification ques-

DEPOSITIONS: Procedures, Strategy and Techniques, designed for use in CLE programs, is the textual abridgement of the looseleaf edition which includes forms on disk. The section and form numbering from the looseleaf edition have been retained in the Professional Education Edition.

tions such as: "Have you understood all the questions you answered?" or "Did you reveal all the facts that you were asked about?" serve as sufficient wrap-up. The deponent may be asked to confirm that all questions have been answered truthfully and accurately. Such questions tighten the transcript and strengthen this tool for impeachment at trial. Some examiners advise the deponent that he has an obligation to supplement any answers given during the deposition should he recall additional information at a later date. Under Federal Rule 26(e), the obligation to supplement responses to formal discovery requests does not ordinarily apply to deposition testimony. *See* Ad.Comm.Notes, Fed.R.Civ.P. 26(e). Where the deponent is an expert, however, that deponent does have an obligation to supplement deposition testimony related to expert opinions.

§ 7.22 Questioning by Other Attorneys

After the lead examiner has completed deposition questioning, all other attorneys present are permitted to examine the deponent. Fed.R.Civ.P. 30(c). No such examination should occur until the lead examiner has completed his or her questioning.

Form 7-1

Question Tree

Case _____   File No. _____

Date of Deposition _____   Deponent. _____

Area of Inquiry: <u>Background</u>

Issue; _____

Question # 1 (Q1):

```
                                          _____• Q3
                                          ( Possible Answer 2
                                          (
                          _____• Q2    (_____• Q3
                          ( Possible Answer 1   Possible Answer 2
                          (
                 Q1       (                _____• Q3
                          (                ( Possible Answer 2
                          (                (
                          (_____• Q2     (_____• Q3
                          Possible Answer 1    Possible Answer 2
```

Issue: _____

Question # 1 (Q1):

```
                                          _____• Q3
                                          ( Possible Answer 2
                                          (
                          _____• Q2    (_____• Q3
                          ( Possible Answer 1   Possible Answer 2
                          (
                 Q1       (                _____• Q3
                          (                ( Possible Answer 2
                          (                (
                          (_____• Q2     (_____• Q3
                          Possible Answer 1    Possible Answer 2
```

Issue: _____

Question # 1 (Q1):

```
                                          _____• Q3
                                          ( Possible Answer 2
                                          (
                          _____• Q2    (_____• Q3
                          ( Possible Answer 1   Possible Answer 2
                          (
                 Q1       (                _____• Q3
                          (                ( Possible Answer 2
                          (                
                          (_____• Q2     (_____• Q3
                          Possible Answer 1    Possible Answer 2
```

Area of Inquiry: <u>Case</u> <u>Facts</u>

Issue: _____

Question # 1 (Q1):

                                _____ • Q2
                        (Possible Answer 1
                        (
        Q1 (
             (
             (_____ • Q2
                  Possible Answer 1

Issue: _____

Question # 1 (Q1):

                                  _____ • Q2
                        (Possible Answer 1
                        (
        Q1 (
             (
             (_____ • Q2
                  Possible Answer 1

Issue: _____

Question # 1 (Q1):

                                  _____ • Q2
                        (Possible Answer 1
                        (
        Q1 (
             (
             (_____ • Q2
                  Possible Answer 1

Issue: _____

Question # 1 (Q1):

                                  _____ • Q2
                        (Possible Answer 1
                        (
        Q1 (
             (
             (_____ • Q2
                  Possible Answer 1

_____ • Q3
(Possible Answer 2
(
(_____ • Q3
  Possible Answer 2
_____ • Q3
(Possible Answer 2
(
(_____ • Q3
  Possible Answer 2

_____ • Q3
(Possible Answer 2
(
(_____ • Q3
  Possible Answer 2
_____ • Q3
(Possible Answer 2
(
(_____ • Q3
  Possible Answer 2

_____ • Q3
(Possible Answer 2
(
(_____ • Q3
  Possible Answer 2
_____ • Q3
(Possible Answer 2
(
(_____ • Q3
  Possible Answer 2

_____ • Q3
(Possible Answer 2
(
(_____ • Q3
  Possible Answer 2
_____ • Q3
(Possible Answer 2
(
(_____ • Q3
  Possible Answer 2

Form 7-1 (continued)
[G20,519]

126

Area of Inquiry: <u>Damages/Injury</u>

Issue: _____

Question # 1 (Q1):

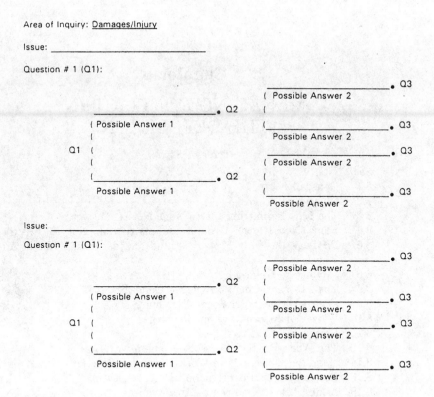

Issue: _____

Question # 1 (Q1):

Chapter 8

MANAGING CONFLICT IN THE DEPOSITION

Table of Sections

---

§ 8.1   Generally

Not surprisingly, attorneys who present their clients for deposition vent their partisan zeal throughout the deposition by obstructing the flow of questions and answers. The examining attorney must understand that the adversary has every incentive to *create* conflict dur-

---

DEPOSITIONS: Procedures, Strategy and Techniques, designed for use in CLE programs, is the textual abridgement of the looseleaf edition which includes forms on disk. The section and form numbering from the looseleaf edition have been retained in the Professional Education Edition.

ing the deposition in order to obstruct the harmful evidence-gathering process. In meeting the presenting attorney's obstructionist tactics, the examiner, however, must resist the temptation to make those tactics the focal point of the examination. Rather, the examiner must *manage* the conflict in a calm but firm manner. Managing the conflict means, at a minimum, neutralizing the obstructionist tactics of the adversary with clear and direct responses based on the law which governs the deposition interaction. In addition, attorneys skilled in the deposition interaction will actually use the conflict to their advantage.

Conflict is likely to arise during the deposition in the following situations: (1) the use of objections to questions; (2) terminating the deposition; and (3) sanctions for deposition abuse. These conflict situations pose different legal and tactical considerations for deposing and presenting attorneys.

§ 8.2 Objections—Generally

Two kinds of objections arise during a deposition. The presenting attorney may object to a question and instruct the witness not to answer. Alternatively, and much more routinely, the presenting attorney objects to a question in order to preserve that objection for trial or for strategic reasons, knowing that the answer must be given subject to the objection.

Although only an objection based on privilege will justify an instruction not to answer, and although the Federal Rules prohibit suggestive or coaching objections, *see* Fed.R.Civ.P. 30(d)(1), presenting attorneys often object on a variety of grounds. In order to handle those objections, the deposing attorney must first understand their underlying purpose. Objections cannot be, and typically are not, used to prevent the deponent from responding to a question. In fact, the Federal Rules expressly provide that evidence objected to at the deposition is taken subject to the objection. Fed.R.Civ.P. 30(c). Why, then, do presenting attorneys bother to

---

object? They do so for two reasons: to prevent waiver of the objections at trial and to control damage done to the deponent.

§ 8.3 The Law Permitting Instructions Not to Answer

The examination of the deponent "may" proceed as permitted at the trial under the rules of evidence. Fed. R.Civ.P. 30(c). But the Federal Rules do not preclude the examiner from deposing a witness in a manner not permitted at trial. *See* Wright & Miller, 8 Federal Practice & Procedure, § 2113. The only absolute constraints on the deposition examination are provided by the rules governing the scope of discovery. Under the Federal Rules, which are copied in most states, the deposing attorney may inquire into any matter:

(1) not privileged;

(2) relevant to the subject matter involved in the pending action;

(3) which relates to any claim or defense asserted by any party;

(4) including the existence, description, nature, custody, condition, location of any books, documents, or other tangible things; and

(5) including the identity and location of persons having knowledge of other discoverable matter. *See* Fed.R.Civ.P. 26(b)(1).

§ 8.4 Scope Not Proper Ground for Instruction Not to Answer

The Rules expressly state that the presenting attorney may not successfully object to the relevance of the questions so long as the information sought appears reasonably calculated to lead to the discovery of admissible evidence. Fed.R.Civ.P. 26(b)(1). Moreover, the Federal Rules expressly provide that objections made at the time of the deposition, including those directed toward the manner of questioning, the evidence presented or

DEPOSITIONS: Procedures, Strategy and Techniques, designed for use in CLE programs, is the textual abridgement of the looseleaf edition which includes forms on disk. The section and form numbering from the looseleaf edition have been retained in the Professional Education Edition.

the conduct of the attorneys, shall be noted by the officer, but may not preclude a response. Instead, evidence objected to during the deposition shall be taken at the deposition, subject to the objections which will be ruled upon if they are raised subsequently at trial. Fed.R.Civ.P. 30(c).

The Federal Rules do permit any attorney to seek a protective order in advance of the deposition limiting the scope or manner of questioning. Fed.R.Civ.P. 26(c). They also allow the presenting attorney to terminate the deposition and seek such a protective order. Fed. R.Civ.P. 30(d)(1). In the absence of such a judicial order, however, the Federal Rules do not permit a presenting attorney to instruct a witness not to answer any questions.

§ 8.5 Privilege the Only Proper Ground for Instruction Not to Answer

The federal rules which are copied in most states make it absolutely clear that, in the absence of a court-ordered evidentiary limitation, the only legitimate basis for an instruction not to answer is privilege. Fed. R.Civ.P. 30(d). An objection based on relevance, the scope of discovery, the form of the question, or the admissibility of the material can never be the basis of an instruction not to answer. If the attorney defending the deposition believes that the questioning constitutes bad faith, harassment, embarrassment or oppression, that attorney's only remedy is to terminate the deposition and seek a court order limiting the questioning. Fed. R.Civ.P. 30(d)(1). Accordingly, as a practical matter, each question must be answered unless it invades a privilege.

§ 8.6 Privileges—Generally

Three different categories of privilege exist: (1) the attorney-client privilege; (2) the work-product privilege; and (3) additional common law privileges.

DEPOSITIONS: Procedures, Strategy and Techniques, designed for use in CLE programs, is the textual abridgement of the looseleaf edition which includes forms on disk. The section and form numbering from the looseleaf edition have been retained in the Professional Education Edition.

§ 8.8 The Attorney–Client Privilege—Generally

The attorney-client privilege, the oldest of privileges known to the common law, is rooted in the belief that if communications between attorneys and clients were discoverable, the client would be reluctant to reveal damaging information to the attorney, and the attorney would be reluctant to counsel the client to alter unlawful conduct. The freezing of information from client to attorney would hamper the attorney's effort to prepare a case or to provide useful advice, while the freezing of information from attorney to client would hamper the attorney's effort to counsel clients in how to obey the law.

The privilege thus has two purposes: (1) it allows attorneys to gather sufficient truthful information in preparation for trial or for counseling and (2) it allows attorneys to use that information to advise clients fully in law-abiding behavior.

§ 8.9 Attorney–Client Privilege—Elements

The purposes of the privilege define its scope. By definition, the claim of privilege requires a showing of the following elements: client, attorney and communication.

First, the person seeking the privilege must be either a client, or someone seeking to become a client, of the attorney with whom the communication was held. Where the client is an individual, this element of the privilege is usually readily satisfied. Where, however, the client is a corporation, a choice of law problem arises. Under federal common law, which governs all federal actions where jurisdiction is not based on diversity alone, the corporate client includes *all* employees within the corporation—not just those in control of its decision-making process—provided that

(1) the employees made the communications to secure legal advice;

DEPOSITIONS: Procedures, Strategy and Techniques, designed for use in CLE programs, is the textual abridgement of the looseleaf edition which includes forms on disk. The section and form numbering from the looseleaf edition have been retained in the Professional Education Edition.

(2) the employees made the communications at the direction of their corporate superiors;

(3) the communications concerned matters within the scope of the employees' employment; and

(4) the employees were made aware that they were being questioned so that the corporation could secure legal advice.

See Upjohn Co. v. United States, 449 U.S. 383, 101 S.Ct. 677, 66 L.Ed.2d 584 (1981).

In *Upjohn,* the Supreme Court rejected the "control-group" theory of the attorney-client privilege in the corporate setting. Under that rejected theory, which is still the law in a majority of states, only communications between an attorney and those individuals within the corporate client who are capable of controlling the future decisions of the corporation are shielded by the attorney-client privilege. This control-group privilege is based on the theory that the attorney-client privilege should protect only advisory communications running from the attorney to the corporation. Because only those in "control" of the corporation have the power to act on an attorney's advice, no need exists to protect communications between an attorney and lower level employees.

In rejecting this view for federal actions not based solely on diversity, the Supreme Court found that the purpose of the attorney-client privilege is not only to protect advisory communications from an attorney to those in control of a corporation, it is also to protect the flow of information from a corporate client to the attorney. Because accurate information relevant to pending or potential litigation often emanates from the lowest level employees, communications from such employees to their attorneys should be shielded as well.

While the Supreme Court as a matter of federal common law rejected the control-group definition of a corporate client, that and alternative state law definitions of the corporate client still control state court actions and pure diversity actions in federal court. Before taking the deposition of a corporate client, the attorney must determine whether the federal or state law of privileges will control, and then determine whether the deponent is a "client" under the governing standards.

Second, the claim of privilege must pertain to a communication to or from an *attorney*. The attorney must be a member of a bar or the subordinate of a member of a bar who is receiving information or giving advice within the scope of his duties as a professional legal adviser. *See e.g.* 8 Wigmore, Evidence, § 2291, at 554 (1961).

Finally, the claim of privilege must, of course, relate to a communication. The communication may be oral or written. But the communication must be made in confidence for the purpose of gaining or giving legal advice.

§ 8.10 Waiver of Attorney–Client Privilege

Even if each of these elements of the attorney-client privilege is present, however, the deposing attorney still has the right to obtain discovery of the privileged material if the privilege has been waived. Waiver can occur either by the client or by the attorney acting on the client's behalf. The attorney-client privilege belongs to the client. Typically, when the client waives the privilege, however, he does so inadvertently at the time the communication is made. The presence of individuals not within the scope of the attorney-client privilege at the time the otherwise privileged communication is given will waive the privilege. Further, the attorney-client privilege does not preclude the discovery of information revealed both to an attorney and independently to someone outside the scope of the privilege.

Although a client may involuntarily waive the privilege, an attorney acting on behalf of the client can do so only by voluntarily consenting to the disclosure. An attorney voluntarily consents to the disclosure of privileged matter when he fails to take reasonable and available steps to prevent disclosure. *See e.g.* Perrignon v.

Bergen Brunswig Corp., 77 F.R.D. 455, 460 (N.D.Cal. 1978). Thus, the burden is placed upon the defending attorney to take affirmative steps to prevent disclosure of the privileged communication.

§ 8.11 Preserving the Privilege

The defending attorney has available three reasonable steps to prevent disclosure at deposition of privileged matter. He may anticipate the questioning which approaches privileged matter and seek a protective order before the deposition. Fed.R.Civ.P. 26(c). Alternatively, the defending attorney may terminate the deposition when questions arise regarding the privileged matter and then seek a protective order. Fed.R.Civ.P. 30(d). Finally, for the sole purpose of avoiding the waiver of an available attorney-client privilege, the attorney may instruct the witness not to answer.

§ 8.12 The Work–Product Doctrine—Generally

Under the work-product doctrine, which is not technically a privilege, the federal courts permit discovery of tangible materials prepared in anticipation of trial by a party or its agent, only if the discovering party can show a substantial need for the materials and that the materials cannot without undue hardship be obtained by alternative means. *See* Fed.R.Civ.P. 26(b)(3). Moreover, the Federal Rules mandate that even if the federal court permits discovery upon this affirmative showing, it must enter a protective order precluding discovery of the mental impressions, conclusions, opinions, or legal theories of the party's attorney or other agent concerning the litigation.

§ 8.14 Handling Objections to Work–Product Protection

If the pursuit of work-product material cannot be anticipated or if the deposing attorney does not wish to tip his hand before the deposition, he should be prepared for a proper objection to his questioning regarding such

DEPOSITIONS: Procedures, Strategy and Techniques, designed for use in CLE programs, is the textual abridgement of the looseleaf edition which includes forms on disk. The section and form numbering from the looseleaf edition have been retained in the Professional Education Edition.

material. In that situation, he should force the defending attorney to state his objection and its grounds. He should voice his disagreement with the objection for the record and do one of the following: (a) terminate the deposition if the challenged questioning is a significant portion of the entire deposition and seek a court order allowing the discovery, (b) phone a judge or magistrate in the district where the deposition is being taken and seek such an order over the phone, or (c) continue with the deposition, stating for the record that the deposition is not completed and will be re-opened after such time as the court may rule on the requested discovery.

In attempting to make the showing necessary to obtain work-product material, the deposing attorney may argue that the material sought (1) was not prepared in anticipation of litigation or trial, (2) was not prepared by an attorney or other agent of a party, (3) includes statements made by the deposing party, (4) is crucial to the case and cannot be obtained by other means or (5) has been disclosed to third-parties who are not agents of the party for purposes of litigation, and thus, the privilege has been waived.

§ 8.16 Responding to an Instruction Not to Answer

If the defending attorney instructs his witness not to answer a deposition question, the deposing attorney should pursue the following course:

First, calmly ensure that the witness has in fact been instructed not to answer.

Second, if the witness has effectively been instructed not to answer, request the defending attorney to state for the record that such instruction has been given. A clear instruction not to answer on the record will be useful should any judicial action be required.

Third, inquire into the scope of the instruction not to answer.

DEPOSITIONS: Procedures, Strategy and Techniques, designed for use in CLE programs, is the textual abridgement of the looseleaf edition which includes forms on disk. The section and form numbering from the looseleaf edition have been retained in the Professional Education Edition.

Fourth, if the defending attorney insists on maintaining a blanket instruction not to answer, consult the law governing the proper use of instructions not to answer. Unless the instruction not to answer is based on a claim of privilege, it is patently improper. If the instruction is based on the attorney-client or other common law privilege, it is not well-taken if the privilege does not apply or if it has been waived. Finally, if the instruction not to answer is based on the work-product doctrine, the deposing attorney should anticipate securing a court order before proceeding with the challenged area of inquiry.

Fifth, if the instruction not to answer is proper, offer to accommodate the objection by inquiring into alternative areas, or by approaching the same area in another way. Even if the instruction not to answer is improper, maintain a conciliatory tone. A calm but firm statement, reminding the defending attorney and the *witness* that the attorney's improper conduct is prolonging the deposition and may force the witness to return on another day, can do more to compel a response than a race to the courthouse.

Finally, if the presenting attorney persists in his improper obstruction of a proper question, the deposing attorney should then consider seeking judicial relief.

§ 8.18   Asking "Bad" Questions—An Advantage

Despite their formal flaws, "bad" questions can be useful tools in discovering facts. If the examining attorney's primary goal in asking a question is to discover facts which may lead to the discovery of additional evidence which is admissible at trial, then the question's improper form may actually foster that goal. A vague question, for example, can induce the witness to provide testimony not even contemplated by the examiner. Similarly, a hypothetical question can induce the witness to volunteer damaging information. Asking a question which the witness is incompetent to answer may induce that witness (or his lawyer) to suggest or state his lack

---

DEPOSITIONS: Procedures, Strategy and Techniques, designed for use in CLE programs, is the textual abridgement of the looseleaf edition which includes forms on disk. The section and form numbering from the looseleaf edition have been retained in the Professional Education Edition.

of knowledge of an entire subject area. The examining attorney, however, must be aware that apart from their value in discovery, objectionable questions do not provide a clean evidentiary record for trial. Thus, by understanding the purposes of an objection, the examining attorney can either avoid the objection by framing a non-objectionable question or can use the objection to his advantage.

§ 8.19   Objections to Control Damage

Most objections at a deposition are neither intended to protect privileged material nor to cure an objectionable question. Rather, the objection is used by the presenting attorney as a device for limiting the damage which may be done to the deponent.

§ 8.20   Response to Coaching the Deponent—Generally

If the examining attorney recognizes the objection to be merely a method of coaching the witness, he should consider the following alternative responses: no response, restating the question verbatim, re-phrase the question, meet the objection, seek judicial relief.

§ 8.21   No Response to Objection

Unless the presenting attorney has expressly instructed the deponent not to respond, the question must be answered despite the objection. The examining attorney should inform the deponent of this rule, preferably once at the start of the deposition. Then, when an objection is raised, the examiner may obtain a response to a pending question simply by making prolonged eye contact with the witness or by nodding the head as if to indicate that the witness should proceed.

The lack of any verbal response to an objection has several advantages. It minimizes the objection, minimizes the conflict, isolates the objecting attorney from the examination and results in a transcript in which the deposition answer is not separated from the deposition question by pages of speeches regarding the objection.

DEPOSITIONS: Procedures, Strategy and Techniques, designed for use in CLE programs, is the textual abridgement of the looseleaf edition which includes forms on disk. The section and form numbering from the looseleaf edition have been retained in the Professional Education Edition.

The lack of any response to the objection, however, can create the impression of passivity or tolerance to frequent subsequent objections. It also has the disadvantage of leaving the transcript less clear than it could be: the deposition question will be separated from the deposition answer by a lawyer's objection to the question. Finally, the absence of any response, of course, cannot cure questions which truly are improper in form.

§ 8.22 Response to Objection—Restate the Question Verbatim

Responding to an objection by merely restating the question verbatim has many of the advantages of no response at all. This method of managing conflict not only minimizes the objection, it helps re-assert the examiner's control over the interaction. Moreover, it has the added advantage of leaving a clean transcript: the answer presumably follows immediately from the restated question.

Merely restating the original question, however, does have the disadvantage of inviting a restatement of the objection. It also may result in the repetition of a question which is improper as to form.

§ 8.23 Response to Objection—Re-phrase the Question

Ideally, all objections as to the form of a deposition question would be well-taken and would result in a re-phrasing of the question so as to make it proper. If the objection is well-taken (*i.e.* the question was vague or compound), the examiner should, without discussion, re-phrase it—maintaining eye contact with the witness. Even if the objection is not well-taken, however, the examiner should consider re-phrasing the next question to cure the alleged defect and returning to the original question later in the deposition.

This approach has the advantage of minimizing the conflict which objections can create. Often, the examin-

DEPOSITIONS: Procedures, Strategy and Techniques, designed for use in CLE programs, is the textual abridgement of the looseleaf edition which includes forms on disk. The section and form numbering from the looseleaf edition have been retained in the Professional Education Edition.

ing attorney will be able to return to the original question at a later time in the deposition without receiving the previous objection. Alternatively, the deposition testimony may render the original question unnecessary.

Re-phrasing a question in response to an objection, however, does have disadvantages. The act of re-phrasing is somewhat of a concession to the adversary. It displays an insecurity in the propriety of the original question. And it allows the presenting attorney to control the form and timing of the deposition questions.

§ 8.24 Response to Objection—Meet the Objection

Lawyers cannot resist a good argument. So when an objection comes at a deposition, the examiner's instinctual response is to fight the objection; confrontation should be a last resort. One lawyer's argument merely breeds another lawyer's response. The result at a deposition is that a relatively innocuous objection can become the focal point of the entire deposition, consuming precious energy, time and transcript pages. Hence, the examiner should resist the temptation to engage the presenter in a speechmaking contest.

Nonetheless, there are situations in which the examiner should make some statement about the objection itself. First, if the objection is patently wrong and such can be demonstrated by the examiner, a response may be appropriate.

Second, if the defending attorney repeatedly objects, a warning may be appropriate. The first warnings should be directed not to the attorney, but to the witness. Statements such as the following are useful: "Mr. Witness, it is now 3:00 o'clock. I had hoped to be able to complete this deposition today. But your attorney insists on interrupting you before you can answer my questions. He understands that despite his objections, you must answer my questions. Still, he insists on prolonging this deposition and is wasting your time."

DEPOSITIONS: Procedures, Strategy and Techniques, designed for use in CLE programs, is the textual abridgement of the looseleaf edition which includes forms on disk. The section and form numbering from the looseleaf edition have been retained in the Professional Education Edition.

Third, the examiner may respond to an objection by asking *the witness* whether he felt the question was unanswerable. The following exchange illustrates this method:

Q. When did you first read the Prospectus?

Defending Attorney: Objection. The question is vague—which prospectus? during what time frame?

Deposing Attorney: (To the witness) Were you incapable of understanding my question? You understood which prospectus I was referring to, didn't you?

A. Yes. I first read the prospectus this morning in preparation for my deposition.

Fourth, the deposing attorney can respond to the objection by using it to confuse the witness, or lead him in different directions. A similar interaction illustrates this approach:

Q. When did you first read the Prospectus?

Defending Attorney: Objection. The question assumes facts not in evidence.

Deposing Attorney: Your objection is well-taken. My question improperly assumes that the witness read the prospectus. I will re-phrase it.

Q. You never read the prospectus, did you?

A. No.

Forms 8–1 thru 8–5 help the examining attorney to manage conflict within the deposition without resorting to judicial relief.

§ 8.25   Response to Objection—Seek Judicial Relief

The deposing attorney confronted with obstructionist objections may also seek a court order compelling deposition answers, Fed.R.Civ.P. 37(a)(2)(B). The deposing attorney may complete or adjourn the deposition before seeking such an order.

*

DEPOSITIONS: Procedures, Strategy and Techniques, designed for use in CLE programs, is the textual abridgement of the looseleaf edition which includes forms on disk. The section and form numbering from the looseleaf edition have been retained in the Professional Education Edition.

Form 8-1

Deposition Objections and Instructions Not to Answer

Objection	Purpose	Is Objection Proper?
1. Privilege	Prevent waiver of privilege.	Yes. Fed.R.Civ.P. 30(d).
2. Scope	Prevent damage control by intimidation or coaching.	No. Fed.R.Civ.P. 80(d).
3. Form—Vague, compound, competency	Prevent waiver of objection, the grounds for which could have been removed at the time of deposition.	No. *see* Fed.R.Civ.P. 30(c).
4. Speaking	To coach the witness.	No. *see* Fed.R.Civ.P. 30(c).
5. Evidentiary Limitation Ordered by Court	Prevent violation of courts order	Yes. Fed.R.Civ.P. 30(d).
6. Bad Faith, annoying, embarrassing or oppressive questioning	To protect the deponent	No. Fed.R.Civ.P. 30(d). Defending Attorney must terminate the deposition and make motion

Form 8-1
[G20,521]

143

Deposition Objections Generally

Objections	Objections	Basis	Response	Follow-up

Form 8-2
[G20,522]

144

Form 8-5

Objection Responses

Objection	Alternative Responses	Response Chosen
(1) Privilege	(1) Accommodate objection by leaving area or approaching another way	
(2) Scope	(1) No response (2) Restate question verbatim (3) Rephrase question (4) Meet objection (5) Seek court relief	
(3) Form	(1) No response (2) Restate question verbatim (3) Rephrase question (4) Meet objection (5) Seek court relief	
(4) Coaching	(1) No response (2) Restate question verbatim (3) Rephrase question (4) Meet objection (5) Seek court relief	

Form 8-5
[G20,523]

145

Chapter 9

DEPOSING ATTORNEY'S POST–DEPOSITION PROCEDURES

Table of Sections

---

§ 9.1 Generally

The deposition does not end when the final question is answered. Rather, the deposition testimony typically is transcribed, submitted to the witness, signed, certified by the officer, and in some cases filed with an appropriate court. Seemingly routine, these procedures can create changes in testimony and problems at trial which will undo an otherwise successful deposition. Accordingly, attorneys must understand these post-deposition procedures and ensure that they are not being used by the adversary in a way which jeopardizes the deposition testimony.

§ 9.2 Preparing a Deposition Summary

As soon as possible after the deposition concludes, the examining attorney should dictate or draft a summary memorandum to the file of the deposition proceedings. Whether or not the transcript of the deposition

DEPOSITIONS: Procedures, Strategy and Techniques, designed for use in CLE programs, is the textual abridgement of the looseleaf edition which includes forms on disk. The section and form numbering from the looseleaf edition have been retained in the Professional Education Edition.

was ordered written, a summary memorandum written in narrative form provides the attorney with an essential tool of review and preparation for subsequent depositions and trial. Form 9–1 provides a format for summarizing the deposition, while Form 9–2 provides a post-deposition checklist.

§ 9.3 Deposition Summary Format

The summary should begin with the names of all present, including the court reporter, the court reporting service and whether the transcript was ordered written. This will help clear what later will be forgotten. Next, a detailed narrative of all information gathered at the deposition follows. The summary need not be written in the order the information was gathered, since the examiner likely shifted around in follow-up and probing. The summary should be a coherent and complete picture of the testimony. The final section of the summary is a detailed statement of witness and attorney demeanor as well as specific comments on the manner in which the deponent responded to questions and the type of witness that the deponent will likely make at trial.

It should be clear that this summary document is an essential part of case development as it reflects not only substantive information, but the examining attorney's work product and thought. These summaries are often referenced for planning settlement or trial.

§ 9.5 Preserving the Right to Change the Transcript

Under Federal Rule 30(e), the deponent no longer has the automatic right to review, change and sign the completed deposition transcript. Instead, that Rule requires the deponent to affirmatively request the opportunity to review, change and sign the transcript. The request must be made during the deposition itself. The right to alter the deposition transcript is a significant one. Accordingly, the examining attorney should never give the deponent the chance to request that right. To

---

DEPOSITIONS: Procedures, Strategy and Techniques, designed for use in CLE programs, is the textual abridgement of the looseleaf edition which includes forms on disk. The section and form numbering from the looseleaf edition have been retained in the Professional Education Edition.

the contrary, the examiner should simply ignore the issue of transcript-review, hoping that the deponent will fail to request that review during the deposition. In most cases, however, the deponent or the deponent's attorney will properly request the opportunity to review, change and sign the deposition transcript.

§ 9.8 Submission of Record to the Witness

If the deponent or any party has requested that the deponent review, change and sign the transcript, the transcript must be

(1) submitted to the witness;

(2) examined by the witness;

(3) read to or by the witness; and

(4) ultimately signed by the witness. Fed.R.Civ.P. 30(e).

The purpose for allowing the witness to examine the record is to allow the witness to make any changes on that record. The rules permit changes in form or substance, provided that the witness provides reasons for making them. Fed.R.Civ.P. 30(e). While it may be improper or imprudent for witnesses to make radical substantive changes in a deposition record, they often do so to erase damaging testimony. The examiner, therefore, should try to prevent such changes whenever possible.

§ 9.9 Obtaining Waiver of Deponent's Rights

The easiest way to prevent the deponent from altering damaging deposition testimony is to get the deponent to waive the right to read and sign the record. The rules provide that examination, reading and signature can all be waived by the *inaction* of the parties and the witness. Fed.R.Civ.P. 30(e). Waiver can be involuntary. If the witness, for whatever reason, does not request the right to sign the deposition, the witness will be deemed to have waived signature. In that instance, the officer certifies in a written attachment to the deposition transcript that no review of the transcript was requested. Fed.R.Civ.P. 30(e), 30(f). Accordingly, the best way for an examining attorney to obtain the deponent's waiver of the right to review, change and sign the transcript is to *ignore* the issue entirely, hoping that the deponent and the other parties will fail to request that right.

§ 9.12 The Substance of Changes

The Federal Rules allow deponents to make any changes "in form or substance" which they desire. Fed. R.Civ.P. 30(e). Those changes are proper even if they totally contradict the original answers. Allen & Co. v. Occidental Petroleum Corp., 49 F.R.D. 337 (S.D.N.Y. 1970). The reasons for the changes need not be convincing. Lugtig v. Thomas, 89 F.R.D. 639, 641 (N.D.Ill. 1981). So long as the proper procedures for making the changes have been followed, the court will not "examine the sufficiency, reasonableness, or legitimacy of the reasons for the changes." Sanford v. CBS, Inc., 594 F.Supp. 713, 714 (N.D.Ill.1984).

If the number or nature of changes make the deposition incomplete or useless, the examining party may move to reopen the examination. Courts will allow the deposing attorney to ask additional questions made necessary by the changed answers, including questions about the reasons for the changes and whether they were made by the witness or by counsel. Sanford v. CBS, Inc., 594 F.Supp. 713, 715 (N.D.Ill.1984). The deponent bears the cost and attorneys fees associated with the reconvening. Lugtig v. Thomas, 89 F.R.D. 639, 642 (N.D.Ill.1981).

§ 9.13 Using the Deponent's Changes at Trial

Even if the examining attorney cannot prevent changes to deposition testimony, he can exploit them at trial. Since the original answer to the deposition question remains part of the deposition record, together with the changes, both the original answers and the changes

DEPOSITIONS: Procedures, Strategy and Techniques, designed for use in CLE programs, is the textual abridgement of the looseleaf edition which includes forms on disk. The section and form numbering from the looseleaf edition have been retained in the Professional Education Edition.

can be read into evidence at trial. Usiak v. New York Tank Barge Co., 299 F.2d 808 (2d Cir.1962). If, for example, the disparity between the original deposition answer and the changed answer is a gross one, and reasons for the disparity are unpersuasive, the deposing attorney may choose to forego a challenge to the change to use them for their tremendous impeachment value at trial.

DEPOSITIONS: Procedures, Strategy and Techniques, designed for use in CLE programs, is the textual abridgement of the looseleaf edition which includes forms on disk. The section and form numbering from the looseleaf edition have been retained in the Professional Education Edition.

Form 9-1

Deposition Summary

Attention Mark	Substantive Notes
to follow up	
to probe	
to clarify	
to reconsider later after other information is gathered	

Form 9-3

Catalogue of Changes

Deponent: _____

Questions	Tr. Pg.	Original Answer	Tr. Pg.	Change	Reason	Notes on Case at Trial

Form 9-3
[G20,525]

Part III

THE DEFENDING PARTY'S PERSPECTIVE

Chapter 10

PREPARING FOR THE DEPOSITION

Table of Sections

---

§ 10.1 Taking an Active Role

Preparation of a witness for deposition entails the attorney's complete analysis of the case. A witness cannot be properly prepared for deposition if the lawyer has not evaluated the legal issues and the witness's position relative to those issues. The attorney should assume the witness's role in order to determine what the adversary will likely seek to bring out through questioning. Proper presentation of a deponent requires com-

---

DEPOSITIONS: Procedures, Strategy and Techniques, designed for use in CLE programs, is the textual abridgement of the looseleaf edition which includes forms on disk. The section and form numbering from the looseleaf edition have been retained in the Professional Education Edition.

pleting an investigation of the case and reviewing the significant aspects of that case with the deponent. The deponent must be prepared with the same degree of care that would be expended to prepare him to testify at trial.

Although a defending attorney may choose not to ask any questions at a deposition, his role is nevertheless an active one. The attorney must listen to all questions asked to ensure proper form and relevant inquiry. Representing the deponent requires the highest level of awareness and preparation since that attorney not only protects the information sought from the deponent, but monitors the information which may reflect the position of all parties. Information revealed at a deposition through a technically improper question may place one or more parties in a precarious or settlement-inducing position. Few attorneys likely want to be responsible for such an improper disclosure.

§ 10.2 Preparation Sessions

In the best of all worlds, an attorney will prepare a deponent for his deposition over several sessions. At the first session, the attorney should give the deponent an overview of the case, explain the deposition process, and provide him with any necessary documents for review.

During subsequent working sessions, the attorney and the deponent should study all of the documents which may be referred to by the examiner at the deposition. In addition, the attorney should recap testimony from any other witness or party who has previously been deposed or who has mentioned the current witness. The attorney should also review the witness's version of the facts in question and should critique the story to ensure its accuracy. The witness should explain the story to the attorney in narrative form to ensure that all information is consistent and accurate. Finally, the deponent's attorney should cross-examine his witness to help solidify the story and ensure its internal consistency.

The final meeting before the deposition should be a time of review. By the time of this final session, the

---

DEPOSITIONS: Procedures, Strategy and Techniques, designed for use in CLE programs, is the textual abridgement of the looseleaf edition which includes forms on disk. The section and form numbering from the looseleaf edition have been retained in the Professional Education Edition.

witness should be confident with and knowledgeable of the deposition process and its relevant procedures.

Many attorneys find these time expectations excessive. Cases vary in their complexity, and depositions vary in the import of potential testimony. As such, there are often depositions for which a deponent can be prepared sufficiently in one or two fairly lengthy (two to four hours) sessions. Several preparation sessions are preferable in a complex matter, when a particular deponent plays a significant role in the litigation, or when particular deposition testimony can be inherently damaging to the case as a whole.

As you consider how often clients frustrate their lawyers at deposition by violating the very rules they have supposedly been taught, consider why clients volunteer information, provide information they do not know and don't follow their attorney's lead. The answer to effective client testimony in the deposition rests, for the most part, in the hands, time and effort of the lawyer. The handy written guides many lawyers give their clients to read prior to the deposition just aren't sufficient to bring the client up to speed for giving effective testimony. Paul M. Lisnek, "Clients Shouldn't Crumble During Depositions," Chicago Daily Law Bulletin, August 9, 1993, p. 6.

In fact, most clients understand the materials, but have no sense of how to integrate the information. This should come as no surprise since most clients have no experience interacting in the type of controlled question and answer exchange a deposition presents. For many, this is the first time they are communicating in an exchange which is no reciprocal in the gathering and offering of information.

A layperson who has never been deposed is most often uncomfortable at the thought of giving formal testimony, and need not only know the rules, but must experience them. Consider the type of rules we want our clients to remember:

DEPOSITIONS: Procedures, Strategy and Techniques, designed for use in CLE programs, is the textual abridgement of the looseleaf edition which includes forms on disk. The section and form numbering from the looseleaf edition have been retained in the Professional Education Edition.

Notes

1. Listen carefully to each question and be certain to answer only the question asked of you.

2. Limit your answer to the question being asked.

3. Do not volunteer any information.

4. Do not explain any of your answers unless requested to do so.

5. If you do not know the answer to a question, simply say that you don't know.

6. Remember that "I don't know" is different from "I don't remember." The first assumes you never had that information and the latter assumes you knew the information at some time in the past.

7. Follow my lead. If I indicate that I do not understand a question, then you should not answer that question.

Now, contrast these rules with what the deponent is usually told by the deposing lawyer at the beginning of any deposition:

1. Be certain you answer each question I ask you because if your answer is not responsive, I will ask that question again.

2. If you need to expand any answer feel free to do so.

3. If you should wish to add anything, feel free to do so.

4. If you need to explain an answer, feel free to do so.

5. If you don't know an answer say so, but I will assume that if you answer my question, that you understood it as I asked it.

It should be clear that the deponent hears instructions at the deposition that are contrary to what was said during the brief preparation session. *id.* It makes perfect sense that clients begin volunteering information and offering extra facts which no question has request-

---

DEPOSITIONS: Procedures, Strategy and Techniques, designed for use in CLE programs, is the textual abridgement of the looseleaf edition which includes forms on disk. The section and form numbering from the looseleaf edition have been retained in the Professional Education Edition.

ed. They react to and go with the rules they heard last, those which come from the deposing lawyer. *id.*

In most cases, the deposing lawyer is friendly and approachable leading many deponents to assist that lawyer. The guard goes down and the mouth opens up. The deponent is most likely relieved that the interaction is manageable. *id.*

Every deponent needs to understand, innately, that control over disclosure in the deposition is an absolute necessity. They must gain trust in the lawyer to bring out information that should be brought out and not to question why the deposing lawyer failed to ask about a certain circumstance. The desire to "help" must be replaced by the pleasure of knowing control. This can be better accomplished through proper preparation. *id.*

§ 10.3 Preparation Session—The Procedure

Proper deposition preparation begins several weeks prior to the deposition. The client/deponent should be brought in to review the process and then to experience a sample deposition. The lawyer may serve as the deposing lawyer for the exercise, or another lawyer in the firm can play that role to permit the client's lawyer to serve in the role of protector. Paul M. Lisnek, "Clients Shouldn't Crumble During Depositions," Chicago Daily Law Bulletin, August 9, 1993, p. 6. Whenever possible, the interaction should be put on videotape so clients can see their mistakes. It is one thing to be told you are volunteering, or do not appear confident. It is quite something else to see the videotape and witness the areas for improvement first hand. *id.*

In many cases, a professional trial consultant may be retained to work with the client. The consultant works, most often, from a communicative perspective. He or she observes carefully and helps the client to deliver the testimony in the most effective manner possible. Consultants never play a role in the substance of the testimony, only in the effectiveness of its delivery. This service can often be hired for no more than a couple

DEPOSITIONS: Procedures, Strategy and Techniques, designed for use in CLE programs, is the textual abridgement of the looseleaf edition which includes forms on disk. The section and form numbering from the looseleaf edition have been retained in the Professional Education Edition.

of thousand dollars, or less. *id.* Where a consultant is used, no commentary should appear on the videotape and a statement as to the work product purpose of the tape should be made both at the beginning and end of the tape. This is important protection to guarding against discovery. Most judges across the country will protect these tapes from being discovered since trial consultants are seen as part of the trial team and the preparation exercise is thus preserved as confidential work product. *id.*

Continue to work with the client until he or she integrates the rules and skills of control and responsiveness. Then repeat the exercise closer to the time of deposition as a means of review and continued skill integration. Only then can the lawyer have some confidence that the client will testify effectively. *id.*

§ 10.4 Establishing Rapport With the Deponent

Rapport between deposing lawyer and deponent, or between lawyer and client is a footprint or result of a natural process; matching and mirroring which occurs between most all human beings. Paul M. Lisnek, "To Build Rapport with Jurors, Forgo Meaning, just do as They Do," Chicago Daily Law Bulletin, May 17, 1993, p. 6. Building rapport with jurors is behavior based. Eric Oliver, *The Human Factor at Work,* Canton, MI, 1993. Paul M. Lisnek and Eric Oliver, *The Complete Litigator,* Andrews Professional Books (Westtown, PA, 1994).

Rapport, or the commonality and alignment between lawyers and jurors, is grounded in conduct, not interpretations. id. The more behaviors we have in common with another person, the greater the likelihood for rapport. As a rule, people are comfortable with others who act similar to themselves. This is the evidence for rapport. Behavioral differences between lawyer and juror suggest an absence of rapport. With awareness and some training in behavioral cues, lawyers can build rapport both consciously and subconsciously with deponents and clients.

DEPOSITIONS: Procedures, Strategy and Techniques, designed for use in CLE programs, is the textual abridgement of the looseleaf edition which includes forms on disk. The section and form numbering from the looseleaf edition have been retained in the Professional Education Edition.

Lawyers typically think that rapport is created through linguistic responses to a behavior. For example, if a deponent acts as though he or she is hot and the lawyer believes the room is muggy, the lawyer may mention the condition. Or, if the deponent appears disturbed by external noise, the lawyer once again raises the issue in the hope of establishing rapport. The flaw is the lawyer's assumption or interpretation about the deponent's behavior. But since explanation and intent merely follow behavior, there are many more equally compelling explanations for that same behavior. *id.* Does discomfort not look like frustration? The best the lawyer can do under this behavioral theory, is to present similar behavioral cues; put the search for meaning aside. *id.*

Simply put, "WHY" is an irrelevant inquiry about human behavior; it produces only fabrication and post-behavior explanation. *id.* There are always more explanations for any particular behavior. So how do we know what a particular behavior means? Answer: we don't. Can the lawyer ever understand when a deponent is in agreement, or not? Answer: yes. Every person has his or her own cues for agreement and rejection. Eric Oliver, *The Human Factor at Work,* (1993). The cues vary from person to person, but each person will *always* use the same cues to signal agreement or disagreement. Lawyers need learn what each deponent's cues are for agreement and disagreement. *id.* We learn this by asking simple "yes" and "no" questions at the start of the deposition. Carefully observe the juror's nonverbal cues, as minute as they may be, and learn them because they will be the same *every time* that deponent agrees or disagrees. *id.*

The challenge is learning what to look for and how to monitor it. The good news is that lawyers can be trained in the skill. Once lawyers learn and understand each juror's cues, they can monitor where each juror is with relation to the case. Paul M. Lisnek, "To Build

---

DEPOSITIONS: Procedures, Strategy and Techniques, designed for use in CLE programs, is the textual abridgement of the looseleaf edition which includes forms on disk. The section and form numbering from the looseleaf edition have been retained in the Professional Education Edition.

Rapport with Jurors, Forgo Meaning, just do as They Do," Chicago Daily Law Bulletin, May 17, 1993, p. 6.

In addition to understanding each deponent's agreement cues, lawyers can work to develop rapport on an other-than-conscious level. Subconscious rapport develops through the appropriate use of mirroring and matching of gestures, vocal tone and word type selection. This conduct creates sameness between lawyer and client or deponent. The technique of mirroring and matching operates at the subconscious level because it occurs naturally. It can be a conscious tool of the master communicator. *id.*

Humans will automatically follow and mirror the behaviors of others. Lawyers can consciously match body position, vocal cues and thinking process. *id.* Subtly matching the body position of persons as they sit in a chair is an extremely effective way of initiating a subconscious level of rapport. Master communicators also match the level of tension in the other person's body and the other person's breathing rate, both of which establish a subconscious bond of rapport. Matching breathing rate further accentuates the same sensations in physiology that the deponent creates. *id.*

The lawyer can also match vocal tone, pitch, volume and speed. A person who speaks loudly is most comfortable with someone else who speaks loudly. If a lawyer speaks very slowly and the deponent speaks very quickly, all will experience discomfort with the dissimilarity. The master communicator matches voice, delivery and language style of others. *id.*

To test for rapport: 1) carefully observe the deponent's posture, body position, vocal tone, and breathing rate; 2) match the cues and observe the mirroring which naturally occurs anyway within 10 to 50 seconds; 3) if the person mirrors back the new behavior, the lawyer will know that rapport has been established. *id.* If the person does not mirror back the shift, this is behavioral evidence that rapport does not yet exist. Repeat the

DEPOSITIONS: Procedures, Strategy and Techniques, designed for use in CLE programs, is the textual abridgement of the looseleaf edition which includes forms on disk. The section and form numbering from the looseleaf edition have been retained in the Professional Education Edition.

exercise from time to time to monitor and measure the existence of rapport between the lawyer and deponent.

§ 10.5 Speaking the Deponent's Language

The preparing attorney should use common English when talking to the deponent and resist any temptation to use legalese. Many witnesses will not admit their inability to understand instructions given to them. Since the attorney spends a great deal of time preparing the witness prior to testifying to ensure that the witness's account is stated clearly, the attorney should monitor the clarity of his own language choice and style.

§ 10.6 Effective Review of the Deposition Rules

Proper preparation of a deponent necessarily includes a complete review of the general rules which govern the deposition, which often entails significant time and expense. Some attorneys attempt to reduce the time required by forwarding to the deponent through the mail a written set of deposition instructions which contain the rules of the interaction. The preparation session is then used to review those instructions.

Most deponents, however, do not understand many of the rules because they lack a frame of reference within which the rules operate. This often explains why witnesses violate the instruction not to volunteer information, and subsequently proceed to give extensive responses beyond the limited requirement of a close-ended question. It is not that the deponent failed to read the rule; it is simply that human nature fails to incorporate the adversarial nature of the interaction as an expectation. The attorney should consider having the client view a videotape of a simulated deposition designed to educate the prospective deponent about depositions.

§ 10.7 Effective Review of the Case

The deponent must understand the components of the case at issue. While some attorneys believe an unprepared deponent to be a good deponent because he

DEPOSITIONS: Procedures, Strategy and Techniques, designed for use in CLE programs, is the textual abridgement of the looseleaf edition which includes forms on disk. The section and form numbering from the looseleaf edition have been retained in the Professional Education Edition.

will more likely need to respond with: "I don't know" to more questions, this view is fallacious. An unprepared deponent *will* disclose a host of information not known even to the presenting attorney. Therefore, reviewing all relevant information serves to highlight areas of potential danger which may arise during the interaction; such review therefore constitutes a protective measure.

Even though the attorney may have discussed the case with the client prior to the preparation session, he should review the relevant issues and update the client on any subsequently uncovered information. This refreshes the client's memory and establishes a mind-set for the deposition. Often, attorneys explain to the witness what has happened in a case, but do not explain the import of the facts. It is worth the attorney's time to review the importance of events with clients, where such exchange is protected, to provide the client with a better frame of reference for handling themselves during the deposition.

The attorney should guard any strategic disclosure with a non-client witness, because the substance of any preparation is discoverable by the other side at the deposition. Uncomfortable is a term insufficient to describe the feeling of an attorney who makes disclosures to a non-client witness because he forgets that such preparation is not protected. This warning is particularly appropriate when an attorney prepares a member of a corporate client who does not fall within the class of individuals protected by the attorney-client privilege. Such preparation is not protected and is discoverable at deposition. Thus, while the attorney should share the importance of case components with a client, a non-client should receive only that information which cannot jeopardize the party's position.

Witness preparation also includes a review of the deponent's knowledge and position. If such information has been discussed over the telephone, through the mail or in written statements prior to the deposition, the attorney should nevertheless review the deponent's story

DEPOSITIONS: Procedures, Strategy and Techniques, designed for use in CLE programs, is the textual abridgement of the looseleaf edition which includes forms on disk. The section and form numbering from the looseleaf edition have been retained in the Professional Education Edition.

during each preparation session. Such a review refreshes the deponent's memory as to prior statements, and may jog the deponent's memory as to additional details and facts. Where a deponent lacks certain information which the attorney expected the deponent to possess, the attorney should inform the deponent as such.

Proper testimony review also includes a review of all relevant documents and tangible objects which may be presented to the witness at deposition. The pleadings, discovery responses, statements, letters, and affidavits which bear the name of the deponent or reflect on his testimony should all be reviewed prior to the deposition.

In reviewing the case with the deponent, the attorney should inform the deponent that every case has three points of view: the deponent's view, the adversary's view, and the truth. In other words, the deponent must understand that a person's testimony is tainted by his own bias or selective memory; other witnesses's view of the case will likely differ. Since all witnesses have their own personal view of the case, the deponent should not be disheartened or angered by conflicting facts or stories which arise during the interaction. The deponent should be advised to tell the truth to the best of his memory and recollection and not to worry about bringing his own story into accord with other versions presented during the deposition.

§ 10.8   Forecasting the Nature of the Deposition Interaction

The preparing attorney should explain to the deponent the nature of the deposition interaction, including varying styles of examining attorneys, the type of questions which may be employed and the scope of the questions that are likely to be asked.

There is probably no better way to explain deposition interaction than putting the deponent through a simulated deposition. The attorney may enlist the assistance of a colleague to play the role of the presenting attorney while the preparing attorney plays the role of

---

DEPOSITIONS: Procedures, Strategy and Techniques, designed for use in CLE programs, is the textual abridgement of the looseleaf edition which includes forms on disk. The section and form numbering from the looseleaf edition have been retained in the Professional Education Edition.

examiner. Asking a series of questions helps the deponent to understand the nature of the interaction rules and his own testimony. Most important, the deponent can review difficult or conflicting areas of the case to ensure a clear story.

The simulated interaction should occur well in advance of the deposition itself. When the exercise occurs too close to the deposition, the deponent is prone to short term memory or hindering fear. The attorney should, whenever possible and certainly in complex or important cases, videotape the simulated interaction and review the videotape with the deponent. Lay deponents are simply too nervous to integrate too much information or analysis just prior to their deposition.

§ 10.9 Effective Review of Deposition Interaction Rules

Prior to understanding the particulars of the testimony to be given, the deponent must understand that deposition interaction operates under rules different from normal conversation. The language choice employed both in preparation and in the deposition is an important consideration because language will be the means by which the deponent constructs a picture of his testimony.

The questions asked will often distort and manipulate the manner in which information is elicited. For example, people shown a film of an auto accident and then asked implicative questions (example: Did you see *THE* broken headlight?) were more likely to report having seen something, whether or not it was actually in the film viewed prior to questioning, than were the subjects who were asked disjunctive questions (example: Did you see *A* broken headlight?). Question form affects not only the answers given by subjects, but also the representations made from their own memory. For example, people gave higher estimates of automobile speed rate when asked: "About how fast were the cars going when they *smashed* into each other?" as opposed to "About

DEPOSITIONS: Procedures, Strategy and Techniques, designed for use in CLE programs, is the textual abridgement of the looseleaf edition which includes forms on disk. The section and form numbering from the looseleaf edition have been retained in the Professional Education Edition.

how fast were the cars going when they *hit* each other?" Even when biased questions do not affect the particular testimony, they can affect the jurors' reconstruction of the presented testimony.

The importance of language choice, style and usage in the creation of testimony in preparation of the witness cannot be overemphasized. The manner in which a particular statement is presented may influence the credibility of that statement and of the witness. Attorneys should spend significant amounts of time with their witnesses to insure that appropriate language is used to relate their accounts.

§ 10.10   The Key Rules of the Interaction

Once the witness understands the nature of the deposition, the attorney should discuss the specific rules employed in the interaction. These rules ideally should be provided to the deponent in writing prior to the deposition. The witness should also be informed that his attorney will be present for the entire deposition to ensure that only proper questions are asked. The deponent need understand that a court reporter will be present to record all of the testimony. Further, the witness should know that each party in the lawsuit will be represented by an attorney, all of whom may ask questions if they so desire. While no judge or jury is present during a deposition, the deponent must understand that the import of his testimony will surface at the time of trial, thereby reflecting on his own credibility. His testimony may also bear upon the potential for settlement of the case.

Whether or not the attorney provides the deponent with a list of rules prior to the preparation session, he should review all of the interaction rules prior to the deposition. The deposition rules of the interaction fall into two groups: those which concern the substance, content and conduct of the interaction, and those which relate to the deponent's preparation for and attitude regarding the deposition.

DEPOSITIONS: Procedures, Strategy and Techniques, designed for use in CLE programs, is the textual abridgement of the looseleaf edition which includes forms on disk. The section and form numbering from the looseleaf edition have been retained in the Professional Education Edition.

Notes

The first category includes rules which relate to the actual gathering, probing and evaluation of information by the examining attorney. In addition to a repeated emphasis to *always* tell the truth, the deponents should be reminded to:

1. Answer only the question asked; do not volunteer any additional information beyond the scope of the question, and do not expand on any previously answered question or seek to educate the examiner.

2. Answer in full, complete sentences.

3. Not guess on any answer, but state only what is actually recalled first-hand. If a specific date, time or place cannot be recalled, then the best approximation should be given, or the deponent should answer "I don't know" or "I don't recall."

4. Summarize where possible when answering a series of questions. So much better if the adversary accepts the summary.

5. Avoid all adjectives and superlatives.

6. Not tip off the examiner as to the existence of documents he does not know about.

7. Beware of questions with double negatives in them.

8. Not testify as to what others know.

9. Not testify as to a state of mind.

10. Not let the examiner testify for the deponent.

11. Not admit understanding a compound question unless there is an understanding of all parts of the question.

12. Pay attention to leading questions, which are those that suggest their own answer.

13. Not adopt the examiner's summary.

14. Take time in answering each question, and think before responding. This gives the deponent's attorney sufficient time to formulate any objections.

DEPOSITIONS: Procedures, Strategy and Techniques, designed for use in CLE programs, is the textual abridgement of the looseleaf edition which includes forms on disk. The section and form numbering from the looseleaf edition have been retained in the Professional Education Edition.

15.   Not answer a question that is not understood; in this event, the deponent should ask for a re-wording or rephrasing of the question.

16.   Not explain the thought process used to formulate a response.

17.   Make it clear whether the response is a paraphrase or a direct quotation, where appropriate.

18.   Look at all relevant documentation before answering any questions.

19.   Not get upset over an inconsistency in responses which may arise, as every witness makes mistakes. Rehabilitation can be performed.

20.   Listen to all objections.   The deponent should not respond to a question when an objection has been stated by his attorney.   The deponent should await the resolution of the objection.

All of these rules affect the gathering and evaluating of deposition testimony pursued by the examining attorney.   Rare is the deponent who knowingly violates these rules.   Rather, violations commonly occur because deponents often forget the adversarial nature of the deposition.   The source of this problem may be an insufficient or undeveloped understanding of the deposition process in the preparation sessions.   The presenting attorney must connect the above rules to the underlying adversarial nature of the interaction.   For example, the deponent must understand that where the examining attorney fails to question on certain issues or facts perhaps deemed to be important by the deponent, it is not the duty of the deponent to bring these issues into the record.   If the deponent's attorney needs such information developed, he or she will do so at the conclusion of the examiner's questioning.

Form 10–1, Witness Preparation—Relating Rules, provides the attorney with a means of relating the rules of the interaction and monitoring the clarification and explanation of these rules to the witness.   Moreover, the

DEPOSITIONS: Procedures, Strategy and Techniques, designed for use in CLE programs, is the textual abridgement of the looseleaf edition which includes forms on disk.   The section and form numbering from the looseleaf edition have been retained in the Professional Education Edition.

witness should understand each of these rules and the form requires attorney notation to this effect.

The rules relating to the deponent's preparation for, and attitude concerning, the deposition process include:

1. Always tell the truth, as the deponent is sworn under oath to do so.

2. Take the legal profession seriously; understand that a deposition is a serious proceeding and the deponent should avoid being overly friendly with the attorneys and should not be accepting of such overtures from the deposing attorney.

3. Never pursue an argument; the attorneys are paid for that service! Always be courteous and avoid using obscenities.

4. Wear plain, neat and comfortable clothing. The deponent should avoid heavy facial make-up and costume jewelry.

5. Use recesses to talk in private with counsel.

6. Remember that answers often serve to score points for the other side.

7. Remember that there is no such thing as "off the record."

8. If possible, never release information until there is an opportunity to go over it with counsel.

These rules advise the deponent that his or her conduct during the deposition is important. The deponent must be courteous and maintain a formal atmosphere. Similarly, permitting the deponent to become friendly with the examining attorney may lead to a violation of conduct rules, such as volunteering information.

These attitude-oriented rules are often not explained to the deponent within the frame-work of the interaction. For example, the deponent should understand that he must be perceived as honest and credible by the examiner and should take this point into consid-

DEPOSITIONS: Procedures, Strategy and Techniques, designed for use in CLE programs, is the textual abridgement of the looseleaf edition which includes forms on disk. The section and form numbering from the looseleaf edition have been retained in the Professional Education Edition.

168

eration when selecting his attire. Similarly, while the "adversary as enemy" framework is often touched upon by attorneys in preparation, the attorney must express to the deponent that excessive cooperation can lead to volunteered information, thereby jeopardizing the case position. The deponent should not be thrown or made uncomfortable if asked whether he was prepared by his attorney prior to the deposition. This question is entitled to a truthful response. There is no reason for a deponent not to disclose the fact that he or she was prepared for the deposition, although substantive content of the preparation session between attorney and client is privileged. This issue is best addressed in the preparation session, preparing the deponent for questions in this regard. Moreover, the deponent should understand that although "off the record" discussions appear to be safe, any information divulged "off the record" may serve to strengthen the adversary's position.

Attorneys must further express to their clients the complexity of the deposition interaction. First, the the client needs to understand that his role is a difficult one. Second, the attorney should explain his protective role in the deposition, *i.e.,* an attorney protects his client deponent through the use of objections. The use of objections assists the attorney to monitor and control the interaction so as to ensure that only proper questions are asked. The attorney has the right to instruct the witness not to answer questions which seem unfair or improper. The attorney or witness may also request a break in the interaction to consult about a question or the direction of the testimony. The presenting attorney also protects the deponent by asking a series of questions at the end of the examiner's questioning deemed to be necessary to clarify or rehabilitate the deponent.

Regardless of the nature and extent of preparation and emphasis of the rules, no rehearsal sufficiently reflects the actual tension or dynamics of the live deposition proceeding. The attorney must judge the amount

DEPOSITIONS: Procedures, Strategy and Techniques, designed for use in CLE programs, is the textual abridgement of the looseleaf edition which includes forms on disk. The section and form numbering from the looseleaf edition have been retained in the Professional Education Edition.

of preparation needed on both a case by case basis and a deponent by deponent basis. Some deponents will require more preparation than others to ensure adherence to the deposition rules. Since these rules are designed to protect not only the deponent, but the position of each party in the interaction by insuring proper disclosure, effective preparation is essential.

§ 10.11 Avoid Powerless Language

Deponent language choice is further highlighted by the distinction between powerful or powerless speech. "Powerless" speech is characterized by a frequent use of intensifiers (example: "so," "very," "too"), empty adjectives (example: "charming," "cute"), hyper-correct grammar, polite forms, gestures, hedges (example: "well," "you know," "I guess"), rising intonation, and a wider range of intonation patterns, *i.e.,* rising questioning intonation in a declarative context. Users of this powerless speech are generally given a negative evaluation by the receivers of such communication.

The absence of these powerless characteristics produces more forceful language which is referred to as "powerful speech." The use of powerless speech can be found in the testimony of both male and female deponents. Professionals (such as doctors, law enforcement agents, etc.) tend to use powerless speech less frequently than do people who are less educated or of lower social status. Nevertheless, powerful speech enhances the credibility of witnesses regardless of their education or social status. Therefore, the attorney should pay close attention to the words employed by that deponent to ensure a presence of clarity, assuredness, and power.

DEPOSITIONS: Procedures, Strategy and Techniques, designed for use in CLE programs, is the textual abridgement of the looseleaf edition which includes forms on disk. The section and form numbering from the looseleaf edition have been retained in the Professional Education Edition.

Form 10-1

Witness Preparation—Relating Rules

Case _____ File _____ Client _____
Deponent: _____

Rule	Stated	Explained	Witness Comprehends (through repetition or example)
1. Understands question			
2. Answers only the question asked			
3. Be responsive			
4. Keep answer simple			
5. Maintain independence			
6. No volunteering			
7. Be confident			
8. Say "I do not know" when needed			
9. Be certain to hear question			
10. Do not be cut off			
11. Keep answers verbal			
12. Answers given assume understood question			
13. Request a break when needed			
14. Supplement answer when necessary			
15. Observe objections as a cue to be aware of the question or answer to which the objection refers			
16. Observe nonverbal cues/signals directed to questions or answers			
17. Tells the truth			

When completed, see if there are any questions still existing in the witness's mind. Give the witness as many examples as possible to clarify each rule.

Form 10-1

[G20,526]

Form 10-2

Witness Preparation—Witness Self–Information Form

Directions: The following form is designed to help you be a better witness at deposition. Human nature encourages us to often say things we cannot be certain of in order to help out. In the deposition, it is essential we say no more than what is asked of us—this form will help you clarify for yourself what you know or do not know. The specific topic or issue has been specified by your attorney.

Complete this form on your own or with the assistance of your attorney, but be certain to review your answers with your attorney before testing at the deposition.

Issue #1 (to be filled in by the attorney): _____

What I know for sure about this issue: _____
_____
_____
_____

How I know what I am certain I know: _____
_____
_____
_____

Why I know what I know for sure: _____
_____
_____
_____

What I do not know (and therefore could not testify to) about this issue: _____
_____
_____
_____

What I do not understand about this issue: _____
_____
_____
_____

Form 10-2
[G20,527]

Issue #2 (to be filled in by the attorney): _____
  What I know for sure about this issue: _____
_____
_____
_____

  How I know what I am certain I know: _____
_____
_____
_____

  Why I know what I know for sure: _____
_____
_____
_____

  What I do not know (and therefore could not testify to) about this issue: _____
_____
_____
_____

  What I do not understand about this issue: _____
_____
_____
_____

Form 10-2 (continued)

[G20,528]

173

Form 10-3

Witness Preparation—Witness Question Sheet

Directions: This form is designed to let you think about some of the questions you may want to ask the attorney. This form enables you to analyze your thoughts.

1. Questions I have concerning the facts of this case: _____

   _____

   _____

   _____

   _____

2. Questions I have concerning how to answer questions properly: _____

   _____

   _____

   _____

   _____

3. Questions I have concerning how to dress/appear at the deposition: _____

   _____

   _____

   _____

4. Questions I have concerning the atmosphere of the deposition: _____

   _____

   _____

   _____

   _____

5. Questions I have concerning the procedures of the deposition: _____

   _____

   _____

   _____

6. Questions I have concerning how I may interact with the attorneys: _____

   _____

   _____

   _____

Form 10-3
[G20,529]

174

7. Questions I have concerning how I act when an objection is made by an attorney: _____

_____

_____

_____

You should give significant consideration to these questions and be certain to discuss these matters with your attorney until all questions have been answered in your mind.

[G20,530]

Form 10-3 (continued)

175

Chapter 11

PRESENTING THE DEPONENT

Table of Sections

---

§ 11.3   Functions of the Presenting Attorney

When representing a deponent or attending depositions of non-client deponents, the attorney should:

(1) monitor the propriety of the interaction;

(2) make timely objections;

(3) instruct the deponent not to answer when appropriate;

(4) use strategic objections; and

(5) decide when to rehabilitate the deponent.

§ 11.4   Monitoring the Propriety of Interaction

Nonexamining attorneys monitor and control the propriety of the interaction by raising objections when necessary during the deposition. Federal Rule 32(d) describes the situations which necessitate an objection during the deposition.

A. *Errors in Deposition Notice.* Subsection 1 of Rule 32(d) states that errors and irregularities in the deposition notice will be waived unless a written objection is properly served upon the party who gave the notice. This Rule precludes a party who fails to appear at a deposition from relying on a technical defect. It is important to note that not all errors

DEPOSITIONS: Procedures, Strategy and Techniques, designed for use in CLE programs, is the textual abridgement of the looseleaf edition which includes forms on disk. The section and form numbering from the looseleaf edition have been retained in the Professional Education Edition.

may give rise to this requirement; listing an incorrect date or location, for example, would not necessarily be an error if the other party or deponent had been notified of the changed time or location.

B. *Disqualification of Examiner.* Subsection 2 of the Rule states that any objection based upon the disqualification of the officer who will take the deposition will be waived unless made before the taking of the deposition begins, or as soon as the disqualification becomes known, or could have been discovered, through reasonable diligence.

C. *Objecting to the Competency, Relevancy or Materiality of Testimony.* Objections to the competency, relevancy or materiality of testimony are not waived by a failure to make such objections before or during the deposition, unless the basis for the objection is one that might have been eliminated if presented at the time of the deposition. Fed. R.Civ.P. 32(d)(3)(A). The Federal Rules eliminate immateriality as an objection, and while relevancy and competency objections are available, only the former is commonly used.

The relevancy objection is guided by Fed. R.Civ.P. 26. The scope of relevance under this rule is much more liberal than the scope of relevance under Federal Rule of Evidence 401. As such, deposition questions seeking information that may not be relevant or admissible at trial are common and proper during discovery; the protecting attorney must nevertheless define those questions which are irrelevant, even under the broad scope of Fed. R.Civ.P. 26.

D. *Other Irregularities.* Irregularities regarding the taking of the deposition, oath or affirmation, conduct of the parties or "errors of any kind which might be obviated, removed or cured if promptly presented" will be waived unless made "seasonably" at the time of deposition. Fed.R.Civ.P. 32(d)(3)(B).

DEPOSITIONS: Procedures, Strategy and Techniques, designed for use in CLE programs, is the textual abridgement of the looseleaf edition which includes forms on disk. The section and form numbering from the looseleaf edition have been retained in the Professional Education Edition.

An attorney who believes he can sidestep the impact of testimony, because the deponent had not been sworn, will be precluded from raising this objection later since seasonable notice and available opportunity existed at the time of deposition which would have removed or cured this error.

The seasonable standard also requires that objections to the form of questions and answers be made at the time of the examination. Where questions could be modified at the time of objection, the presenting attorney must register an objection and permit a cure. This objection refers to problems of question and form such as ambiguity, complexity, confusing, or otherwise inappropriate questions. The standard would also reflect non-responsive answers.

Some aggressive presenting attorneys will object when they hear leading questions during the deposition. This response is inappropriate; the deponent is often adverse to the examiner permitting the use of leading questions. The presenting attorney is advised to recognize a distinction between appropriately used leading questions and improper argumentative or hostile questions.

§ 11.6 Instructing the Deponent Not to Answer

Since in most cases registering an objection at deposition will be sufficient to preclude the information from coming in at the time of trial as impeachment, most questions will be answered at deposition subject to the objection. However, there are times when an attorney will register an objection and instruct the deponent not to answer the question. Instructions not to answer a deposition question are proper only in two situations: where the information sought is privileged or where the question invades an evidentiary limitation ordered by the court. Fed.R. 30(d)(1). An instruction not to answer is not proper based on the irrelevance of the question. If the defending attorney genuinely believes

DEPOSITIONS: Procedures, Strategy and Techniques, designed for use in CLE programs, is the textual abridgement of the looseleaf edition which includes forms on disk. The section and form numbering from the looseleaf edition have been retained in the Professional Education Edition.

that a series of questions has been conducted in bad faith, with an intent to unduly harass, embarrass or oppress the witness, the attorney may terminate the deposition and seek an order from the court limiting the examination. *See, e.g.,* Ralston Purina Company v. McFarland, 550 F.2d 967, 973 (4th Cir.1977).

§ 11.7 Deciding to Instruct Not to Answer

In deciding whether to instruct the witness not to answer, attorneys strike a balance between the inconvenience of that witness's disclosure of information which will be precluded at trial based upon objection at deposition and the harm caused by having to reconvene the deposition to get information determined to be appropriate. (W.R. Grace & Company v. Pullman, Inc., 74 F.R.D. 80, 84 (W.D.Okl.1977)).

Protecting attorneys must remember that they have no right to instruct a non-client deponent not to answer a question. The protecting attorney may make a suggestion to the witness that such a question is likely inappropriate and need not be answered. The non-client witness, however, will make such a decision based on his own judgment. Non-client witnesses thus may attend a deposition with their own attorney present. In fact, the protecting attorney may be violating an ethical disciplinary rule by advising a non-client deponent in a legal way other than encouraging that deponent to seek legal representation. (*See,* Code of Professional Responsibility DR7–104(2)).[1]

§ 11.8 Responding to an Instruction Not to Answer

The examiner may respond to an instruction not to answer a question in two ways. First, the attorney may simply drop the issue and move on. Second, the attor-

---

1. "During the course of his representation of a client, a lawyer shall not ... 2. Give advice to a person who is not represented by a lawyer, other than the advice to secure counsel, if the interests of such person are or have a reasonable possibility of being in conflict with the interests of his client."

DEPOSITIONS: Procedures, Strategy and Techniques, designed for use in CLE programs, is the textual abridgement of the looseleaf edition which includes forms on disk. The section and form numbering from the looseleaf edition have been retained in the Professional Education Edition.

ney may turn to the deponent and ask whether that person will answer the question or not, based on the advice of his attorney. Where the examiner seems to create an interference by beginning to explain implications of certifying questions based upon objection, the presenting attorney is urged to step in and limit the examiner's lectures. Failure to do this may make uncomfortable the deponent who fears personal implications. The protecting attorney should be aware that the examiner may nevertheless attempt to repeat the question in a different form or at a different time or may work to discuss, on or off the record, the need to have the question answered. The presenter may stick by his decision, but must have a legitimate basis for preventing disclosure.

§ 11.9 Objections as Strategy

Every objection made in a deposition should be supported by a legitimate foundation, either relevant to the form of the question, or its substance. The demeanor with which the objection is made, however, can serve a strategic purpose beyond the technical reason for the objection. Conducted within the bounds of ethical and civil behavior, an objection can often disrupt the train of thought of an examiner who may not pursue an answer after an objection is registered. The examiner may see his own question as improper and fear admitting that he sees the problem. There may be times when the examiner is not sure of the propriety of the question being asked, and an objection made at the right time may be sufficient to shift the approach of the examiner.

The mere registering of objections is usually seen by the deponent as a signal that something is wrong with the question or subsequent answer. Clients are best advised during deposition preparation that the registering of an objection should be seen as a signal that encourages them to maintain guard at that time.

Any non-examining attorney has the right to register objections to any questions posed to a deponent,

DEPOSITIONS: Procedures, Strategy and Techniques, designed for use in CLE programs, is the textual abridgement of the looseleaf edition which includes forms on disk. The section and form numbering from the looseleaf edition have been retained in the Professional Education Edition.

whether or not that deponent is a client. The objection may cause the examiner to lose his train of thought, or even to become argumentative. The objection thus may destroy the rapport which the examiner is trying to build.

See § 10.4 on the development of rapport with the deponent.

Protecting attorneys should nevertheless be aware that registering an objection can induce an attorney to seek even more information than originally intended. For example, where objection is made to question form, the examiner may respond by asking a series of foundational or otherwise probing questions to establish the relevancy of the question or suggest why the form may be proper. As such, even more detailed information than was originally sought will come of record, all of which could have been avoided by not registering the objection to the initial question. Therefore, protecting attorneys must consider the negative implications of registering objections.

*

DEPOSITIONS: Procedures, Strategy and Techniques, designed for use in CLE programs, is the textual abridgement of the looseleaf edition which includes forms on disk. The section and form numbering from the looseleaf edition have been retained in the Professional Education Edition.

Chapter 12

NONVERBAL COMMUNICATION IN THE DEPOSITION

Table of Sections

---

§ 12.1   The Significance of Nonverbal Cues

The nonverbal cues which accompany messages from the protecting attorney are as significant as those communicated by the examining attorney. *See* Chapter 6. The tone of voice used by the presenting attorney to register objections or protect the deponent, and the way in which the protecting attorney controls and moves his or her body, all affect the atmosphere of the interaction and potential testimony of the deponent.

§ 12.2   Use of Voice

The protecting attorney should be aware that the tone of voice used when interacting with other participants in the deposition greatly shapes the interaction atmosphere.

Where the examiner steps out of bounds in questioning propriety or is otherwise hostile or unfair to the deponent, the protecting attorney can utilize an aggressive or stern vocal tone to warn the examiner to observe procedural rules. An examiner who sees that a protecting attorney means business will often modify his behavior.

Where other attorneys present at the deposition consistently register objections or can otherwise interrupt the interaction, the protecting attorney can utilize vocal tone to put them aback as well. In effect, all participants, other than the deponent, can be alerted through strong vocal tone that the protecting attorney is closely monitoring and observing the interaction to ensure adherence to the rules.

Aggressive vocal tone may be the most useful means of signaling a deponent that he is violating a procedural rule. The deponent, when volunteering information, will take heed when the attorney aggressively warns, "you've answered the question!" Some deponents need strong urging before they finally realize the error of their ways. The protecting attorney should never hesitate to use an aggressive tone when a deponent gives answers beyond the question asked, including potentially harmful information.

§ 12.3 Effective Body Language

The protecting attorney's posture affects the atmosphere and direction of the testimony. Body positioning also reflects the alertness of the protecting attorney as well. An attorney who leans back comfortably and casually will create an impression of comfort to the other participants and may become passive in his own monitoring of the interaction. Such a position may be acceptable during preliminary or background questioning, but the protecting attorney should always sit straight up to remain aware.

Even while sitting straight up, an attorney may lean forward in his chair, signalling concern and heightened attention. Such behavior can have the same effect as registering an objection; it diverts the examining attorney's direction of questioning. When combined with a stare or otherwise strong eye contact to the examiner, the attorney in an aggressively leaning forward position sends a strong signal to the examiner that questions must be appropriate or that he may be treading on inappropriate grounds.

Similarly, by leaning forward and making eye contact with the deponent, the protecting attorney sends a signal to the deponent that his answer or subsequent answers must be guarded. A deponent who is prepared during the preparation session to watch the body positioning of his attorney will pick up on the cues of caution and monitor his responses.

§ 12.6 Making a Record

Most attorneys recognize that nonverbal signals or cues are not recorded on the transcript by the court reporter. As such, nonverbal communication provides a powerful way of controlling the interaction. The attorney should never forget his ability to place on to the record inappropriate conduct which could in itself be the basis for sanctions against the attorney utilizing such conduct. For example, a frustrated examiner who consistently pounds his fist on the table and uses an aggressive and loud tone of voice may scare a deponent into making a disclosure. While the record would not illustrate such behavior, the protecting attorney can state on the record: "Mr. Examiner, there is no need for you to pound your fist on the table and raise your tone of voice to a level which is clearly upsetting to the deponent and unsettling to myself as well." Such a statement will likely produce a swift modification in behavior by the examiner who realizes that subsequent tactics will be exposed by this observant competent attorney.

*

DEPOSITIONS: Procedures, Strategy and Techniques, designed for use in CLE programs, is the textual abridgement of the looseleaf edition which includes forms on disk. The section and form numbering from the looseleaf edition have been retained in the Professional Education Edition.

Chapter 15

THE DEPOSITION OF AN
EXPERT WITNESS

Table of Sections

---

§ 15.1 The Expert Witness

Under federal rules 702, 703 and 705, which have been replicated throughout the states, a witness may offer opinion testimony if that witness has "specialized knowledge" which will assist the trier of fact to understand the evidence or to determine a fact in issue. In assisting the trier of fact, an expert witness may offer an opinion on the ultimate facts at issue in the case. Moreover, a qualified expert may base an opinion regarding an ultimate issue in the case upon information that would not itself be admissible at trial. *See, e.g.,* Fed. R.Evid. 705. As a result of these relaxed standards for expert qualifications and for the bases of their opinions, litigants commonly use experts in all types of civil litigation not only to support their theories of the case. Indeed, expert witnesses have become the rule rather than the exception in civil litigation.

In light of the heightened role which experts play in litigation, the pre-trial expert discovery process is critical. Indeed, the evidentiary rules which permit an expert to offer opinions based on inadmissible material *depend* upon procedural rules which permit penetrating pre-trial discovery. The expert's deposition thus has become one of the most important points in civil litigation.

DEPOSITIONS: Procedures, Strategy and Techniques, designed for use in CLE programs, is the textual abridgement of the looseleaf edition which includes forms on disk. The section and form numbering from the looseleaf edition have been retained in the Professional Education Edition.

§ 15.2 Types of Experts

There are two kinds of experts:

1. *Testifying Experts.* Persons who may be used at trial to provide expert opinion evidence are considered to be testifying experts. Such witnesses include persons retained or specially employed to provide expert testimony in the particular case and employees of a party whose duties regularly involve giving expert testimony. A party may depose any such person who has been identified as an expert whose opinions may be presented at trial. *See, e.g.,* 26(a)(2); 26(b)(4)(A).

2. *Consulting Experts.* A consulting expert is an expert who has been retained by a party in anticipation of litigation or trial, but who is not expected to be called as a trial witness. Discovery through interrogatories or depositions may be obtained from such consulting experts only upon a showing of "exceptional circumstances" amounting to substantial need or undue hardship. *See, e.g.,* Fed.R.Civ.P. 26(b)(4)(B).

§ 15.3 The Disclosure Regime for Testifying Experts

Whether or not the litigation is governed by a regime of automatic prompt disclosure, the following information generally must be disclosed prior to the expert's deposition:

1. A complete statement of all opinions to be expressed;

2. The basis and reasons for each opinion to be expressed;

3. The information considered by the expert in forming the opinions;

4. Exhibits supporting the opinions;

5. The expert's qualifications, including publications and prior testimony; and

DEPOSITIONS: Procedures, Strategy and Techniques, designed for use in CLE programs, is the textual abridgement of the looseleaf edition which includes forms on disk. The section and form numbering from the looseleaf edition have been retained in the Professional Education Edition.

6. The compensation to be paid to the expert. *See, e.g.,* Fed.R.Civ.P. 26(a)(2)(B). The examining attorney must insist on obtaining this type of information about the expert before the expert's deposition. *See* Fed.R.Civ.P. 26(b)(4)(A). Because expert discovery typically follows fact discovery, the examining and defending attorney should have access to all of the significant evidence in the case prior to any expert's deposition.

§ 15.4 Deposing the Expert

In addition to following the procedures, strategies and techniques which are effective in the deposition of a lay witness, the examining attorney should follow the additional guidelines which are unique to the expert deposition.

1. Do not be intimidated by a perceived relative lack of specialized knowledge.

Even the most experienced litigator may feel intimidated by a designated expert's apparent degree of specialized knowledge. Trial lawyers often believe that they cannot keep up with experts in fields as specialized as a structural engineering, accounting or medicine. More significantly, deposing attorneys frequently feel that they will be unable to obtain admissions from a witness who can retreat into the language of his or her own expertise.

The examiner however must reject the temptation to concede to the expert any superiority of knowledge, even in the expert's area of expertise. Expert witnesses rarely have enough specialized knowledge of the exact issues at stake in the litigation to provide an opinion without further research. Instead, experts typically are hired for their general field of expertise and are then asked to apply their general expertise to the narrow issue or issues in the case. As such, experts do, or at least should, spend a great deal of time getting up to speed in the narrow area on which they have been asked to render an opinion. For example, an expert in retail

DEPOSITIONS: Procedures, Strategy and Techniques, designed for use in CLE programs, is the textual abridgement of the looseleaf edition which includes forms on disk. The section and form numbering from the looseleaf edition have been retained in the Professional Education Edition.

Notes

marketing may be hired to provide an opinion with regard to the relevance of the Christmas season to a department store's annual sales projections. Although that expert may have an impressive curriculum vitae and may have a lifetime of retail experience, it is unlikely that the expert can offer an opinion regarding the importance of Christmas sales in the particular industry, location and retail store at issue in the case without significant additional research. If that expert must do additional research to offer a sound opinion in the case, there is no reason why the deposing attorney cannot match the expert's knowledge of the precise issues in the case with the same degree of research.

To take another example from the legal profession, suppose a securities lawyer were asked to provide an expert opinion regarding an attorney's obligations to the client in a public offering. That lawyer may well have tremendous knowledge and experience regarding the proper regime involved in making a public offering. Yet, it is unlikely that the lawyer, absent additional research, would have the same degree of specialized knowledge regarding the precise issue of the interpretation and application of the rules of professional conduct to the relationship between an attorney to a client in that situation. Accordingly, the examining attorney in type of case can obtain as much specialized knowledge of the issues at stake in the litigation as any purported expert.

2. Prepare

Preparation is the single most important ingredient in any effective deposition. Preparation is particularly important, however, when the deponent is an expert who will attempt to offer opinions on the ultimate issues in the case.

Preparation for an expert's deposition should be built upon a foundation of preparation from prior discovery. Prior to the expert discovery phase, the deposing attorney should have thoroughly researched the law governing the case, and have developed a contention

DEPOSITIONS: Procedures, Strategy and Techniques, designed for use in CLE programs, is the textual abridgement of the looseleaf edition which includes forms on disk. The section and form numbering from the looseleaf edition have been retained in the Professional Education Edition.

outline which clearly articulates the ultimate facts which the defendant must prove in order to prevail and the ultimate facts which the defendant must prove in order to establish any affirmative defenses. In addition, the examining attorney should be able to organize the results of all prior fact discovery in a way that develops the evidentiary support for the ultimate facts which are at issue in the case. Once fact discovery is completed and incorporated into an evolving contention outline, preparation for the expert deposition can begin.

Typically, the examining attorney will have the following information regarding an expert deponent in advance of the deposition: (1) the identity of the expert; (2) a written report containing a complete statement of all of the expert's opinions and their bases; (3) the information considered by the deponent in forming the expert opinions; (4) exhibits which will be used to summarize or to support the expert's opinions; (5) the qualifications of the witness, including publications in the prior ten years and testimony given in the prior four years; and (6) the compensation to be paid the expert. *See, e.g.,* Fed.R.Civ. 26(a)(2). The deposing attorney should view these required disclosures as the starting point, not the completion, of preparation for the expert's deposition.

First, the deposing attorney should use the information obtained in these required disclosures to pursue additional sources of discovery about the expert. The expert's qualifications usually are set forth in a curriculum vitae which includes the expert's education, employment, publications, prior testimony and presentations. Whenever possible, the examining attorney should determine the accuracy of the statements made in the expert's curriculum vitae. The representations made in the expert's curriculum vitae are not always accurate; they are frequently exaggerations or inflations of the expert's experiences.

The deposing attorney should obtain copies of the expert's prior work, including publications and, if possi-

---

DEPOSITIONS: Procedures, Strategy and Techniques, designed for use in CLE programs, is the textual abridgement of the looseleaf edition which includes forms on disk. The section and form numbering from the looseleaf edition have been retained in the Professional Education Edition.

Notes

ble, previous testimony. Publications are relatively easy to find. Prior testimony is more difficult. In attempting to get copies of that prior testimony, the examining attorney should research the history of the case in which that testimony was offered. If the case reached trial and resulted in a published opinion, the examining attorney can determine whether the court commented in any way on the expert's opinion in the case. If the case reached trial, but did not result in any published opinion addressing the expert's testimony, the examining attorney should nonetheless find out who the lawyers were in, the prior litigation and contact those attorneys for copies of the expert's trial or deposition testimony. Counsel usually are willing to provide copies of the relevant expert testimony. Lawyers also tend to be forthcoming about their general impressions of the expert's strengths and weaknesses.

A transcript of an expert's prior trial or deposition testimony can be an invaluable tool in preparing for any subsequent deposition of that same expert. The examining attorney can rely upon the transcript not only to organize the deposition, but also to anticipate the expert's responses to similar questions. Because the expert's background should not change dramatically from one deposition to the next, the deposing attorney can take advantage of prior testimony offered by that expert to eliminate needless inquiry and to focus on effective lines of questioning. Prior testimony also can be used as a basis for attacking the expert's credibility. That prior testimony may be inconsistent with the expert's current testimony. On the other hand, the overall pattern of the expert's prior testimony may reflect the expert's general biases. For example, the witness may invariable testify on behalf of management in disputes with unions, or testify on behalf of injured plaintiffs in medical malpractice cases on or behalf of the securities industry in securities arbitrations. This type of history of one-sided testimony may provide an effective basis for challenging the expert's independent judgment in any given case.

After the examining attorney acquires as much information about the expert as is possible, that attorney must begin the process of getting up to speed in the expert's discipline. This is not an impossible task. The examiner should consult the basic texts in the expert's field and should obtain a glossary of the jargon used in that field. The examining attorney's own consulting or testifying expert, of course, can be extremely helpful in this process. Armed with a basic general understanding of the field and its key terms of art, the examining attorney should focus intensely on the narrow issue in the case. The resolution of the issues in the case typically involves the application of a precise aspect of the expert's knowledge and a precise aspect of the expert's field. The examiner can and should learn everything about that precise portion of the field. The examiner then will be on a level playing field with the expert, and will not lose valuable admissions due to a relative lack of knowledge.

Once the examiner has a complete understanding of the expert's background and of the field of expertise involved in the case, that examiner should begin to craft a deposition plan. That plan should be rooted, as with any deposition, in a firm understanding of the ultimate facts at issue in the case. That understanding should give rise to a "wish list" for the expert's deposition. If the examiner had his or her wish, what would the expert deponent say or admit? The wish list should be precise. Once that list is carefully constructed, the examiner can begin to craft questions and lines of questioning which are specifically designed to elicit the desired responses. The examiner even can assume that expert will *not* make the wished-for statements or admissions. The trick of any effective deposition is to design a series of questions which leads the witness *close* to those statements or admissions.

Naturally, the wish-list and the technique of obtaining desired admissions will vary from case to case, and from examiner to examiner. In all cases involving ex-

DEPOSITIONS: Procedures, Strategy and Techniques, designed for use in CLE programs, is the textual abridgement of the looseleaf edition which includes forms on disk. The section and form numbering from the looseleaf edition have been retained in the Professional Education Edition.

perts, however, the examiner should endeavor to establish the following common points:

(1) The expert is not qualified to render an opinion in the case, because

   (a) the expert generally lacks sufficient experience, education or training; or

   (b) the expert lacks sufficient experience, education or training in the precise issues at stake in the litigation; or

   (c) the expert will not assist the trier of fact because the expert will offer a pure legal opinion which is within the sole province of the judge, or will offer an opinion already within the ken of the average juror.

(2) The expert is biased because,

   (a) the expert's compensation depends upon an opinion favoring the party sponsoring that expert;

   (b) the expert generally favors the same side in all cases;

   (c) the expert is related to parties or interested persons in the litigation;

   (d) the expert's career or professional development depends on an opinion favoring the sponsoring party;

   (e) the expert has established ties to the sponsoring party or its lawyers.

(3) The expert's opinions in the case are inconsistent with

   (a) the expert's prior testimony;

   (b) the expert's prior publications;

   (c) the expert's prior presentations; or

   (d) the expert's prior testimony, or positions, in this very case.

(4) The expert's opinions are based on facts which do not exist in this case;

DEPOSITIONS: Procedures, Strategy and Techniques, designed for use in CLE programs, is the textual abridgement of the looseleaf edition which includes forms on disk. The section and form numbering from the looseleaf edition have been retained in the Professional Education Edition.

(5) The expert's opinions would be different if the expert assumed the existence of the facts in the case;

(6) The expert has no opinions with regard to some of the ultimate issues in the case, and will not offer any such opinions at trial;

(7) The expert's understanding of the facts of the case is based (only) on communications which the expert has had with the sponsoring attorney;

(8) The expert acknowledges that the adversary's expert is considered to be an expert in his or her field;

(9) The expert acknowledges the validity of all or some of the assumptions and techniques upon which the adversary's expert opinion is based, and

(10) The expert agrees with all or some of the opinions rendered by the adversary's expert.

These areas of inquiry, which are common to most expert depositions, should be included in a flexible outline for the expert's deposition. They must, of course, be supplemented by areas of questioning which are designed to elicit admissions regarding the precise issues in the case. The outline should be inclusive so that no area of inquiry is overlooked. Yet, the outline should be flexible so that the examiner feels free to listen carefully to the expert's answers and to follow those answers with questions designed to lead to admissions.

3. Employ deposition techniques used for non-experts.

Although the nature of the testimony which the expert offers is fundamentally different from that of an occurrence witness, the examiner should not adopt new or uncomfortable questioning techniques. Many attorneys mistake the expert witness for a neutral mediator who will offer nonpartisan testimony. To the contrary, an expert deponent typically is an adverse or even hos-

---

DEPOSITIONS: Procedures, Strategy and Techniques, designed for use in CLE programs, is the textual abridgement of the looseleaf edition which includes forms on disk. The section and form numbering from the looseleaf edition have been retained in the Professional Education Edition.

tile witness. The expert can and should be asked leading questions designed to obtain a desired admission.
The examiner must *control* the deposition and the expert
at all times. The examiner thus should use posturing,
eye-contact and other methods of non-verbal communication to maintain that control.

4. Base questions on a thorough understanding of the detailed facts in the case.

Even if an expert witness has developed a finely-
tailored opinion in the case, it is unlikely that the
witness knows or understands all of the significant facts
or the evidence adduced in prior discovery. The examiner *must* know and understand these facts and the fruits
of prior discovery.

Based on a knowledge of the key facts in the case,
the examiner can frame leading questions which assume
those facts. Moreover, the examiner can employ these
facts in creating hypothetical questions for the witness
which challenge the application of the witness' general
opinions to the assumed facts in the hypothetical. The
so-called hypothetical facts, of course, are not hypothetical at all. They are the real facts in the case.

For example, suppose in a breach of fiduciary duty
suit brought against the Board of Directors of a major
corporation that the Board's expert opines that the
Board made its decision to reject a hostile acquisition
after a "reasonable" inquiry. The examiner knows, but
the expert does not know, that the Board's decision was
reached without the benefit of a written report from the
company's chief financial officer. The examiner should
test the expert's general opinion with a hypothetical.
The tone of the question should suggest to the expert
that the facts built into the question are merely hypothetical. But those facts should be real. The examiner
might ask: Dr. Jones, I am curious whether your opinion would be the same if the Board in this case had acted
without the benefit of a report from the company's chief

DEPOSITIONS: Procedures, Strategy and Techniques, designed for use in CLE programs, is the textual
abridgement of the looseleaf edition which includes forms on disk. The section and form numbering
from the looseleaf edition have been retained in the Professional Education Edition.

financial officer. Alternatively, the examiner might inquire along these lines:

(1) Dr. Jones, was it reasonable and customary in the industry for Board members to conduct a thorough inquiry before reaching their decision to reject a hostile acquisition offer? The expert must answer "yes," because in negative would require the expert to admit that the industry standards did not require a thorough inquiry;

(2) And Dr. Jones, was it reasonable and customary in the industry for that thorough inquiry to include reviewing any reports submitted by financial advisers? It is difficult for the expert to answer this question in the negative because the question assumes that reports have been submitted and asks whether "reviewing" them was customary. In fact, the examiner should use voice inflection to emphasize the word "reviewing" so that the witness focuses on whether it was customary to *review* submitted reports, rather than upon whether it was customary to prepare them. The expert cannot opine that Board members typically do not review reports which they receive. Surely, the standard of care in the industry cannot be satisfied if Board members ignore financial advice.

This series of questions can take many different forms. But those forms all proceed from a thorough and precise understanding of the facts, which facts can then be used in various ways as part of leading, hypothetical-sounding questions.

5. Never assume that the expert is qualified.

Examining attorneys frequently feel overwhelmed by the credentials of the adversary's designated expert. The expert's lengthy curriculum vitae commonly contains a wealth of education, experience and publications. The examiner naturally is tempted to concede that the expert is qualified to render an opinion in the case. The

DEPOSITIONS: Procedures, Strategy and Techniques, designed for use in CLE programs, is the textual abridgement of the looseleaf edition which includes forms on disk. The section and form numbering from the looseleaf edition have been retained in the Professional Education Edition.

temptation is particularly great because the standards governing the qualifications of expert witnesses are not difficult to meet.

The examiner, however, should not concede that the expert is qualified to offer an opinion in the case. The examiner instead should use the expert's curriculum vitae as a jumping-off point for probing questions about the expert's qualifications. First, the expert should ask whether the statements made in the curriculum vitae are accurate. If, in fact, they are not accurate, the expert's statement under oath that they are accurate can provide an excellent basis for attacking the expert's credibility.

Second, the examiner should ask the expert whether the curriculum vitae is current. Typically, the expert's resume will not reflect the expert's most recent activities and publications, some of which may be relevant to the expert's opinions in the case. If the expert testifies to additional activities not stated on the resume, the examiner, of course, should explore the nature of those activities. The examiner, on the record, also should request the expert to produce useable copies of publications or unpublished works in progress which relate to the expert's opinion in the case.

Third, the examiner should "lock the expert in" to the qualifications described in the resume or curriculum vitae. The following question can be asked in a variety of forms: "Dr. Jones, do you have any credentials which would qualify you to render an opinion in this case which are not reflected in your curriculum vitae?" The expert must be forced to give the examiner a *complete* statement of all of the expert's purported qualifications.

Fourth, after the examiner obtains a complete statement of the expert's purported qualifications, the examiner should walk through those qualifications one at a time with the expert. But the exploration of those purported qualifications must be controlled by the examiner. The exploration should not allow the expert to

---

DEPOSITIONS: Procedures, Strategy and Techniques, designed for use in CLE programs, is the textual abridgement of the looseleaf edition which includes forms on disk. The section and form numbering from the looseleaf edition have been retained in the Professional Education Edition.

offer gratuitous general statements of the expert's own superior credentials. To the contrary, the examiner must focus the exploration of the expert's credentials on this question: How does each purported credential provide the expert with the expertise to offer an opinion on the precise issue *in this case?* Faced with that narrow question, the expert's credentials tend to melt away. Invariably, the expert's curriculum will be filled with a wide range of work. Some of that work will have nothing to do with the field of expertise for which the expert has been called. Other portions of the expert's work may be within the relevant field of expertise, but will not address the precise issues in the case. Indeed, rarely will an expert have an experience or a publication which involves the core issue in the case.

The examiner, therefore, must press the expert to testify as to how each of the credentials listed on the resume has given the expert the skill to offer an opinion in the case. The examiner cannot accept general responses. Instead, the examiner must force the expert to link the purported credential to the opinions in the litigation. If the credential is a publication, the examiner should ask the expert to point to those passages in the publication which the expert believes relate to the issues in the case. The examiner again should lock the expert in, by leading the expert to state that the passages which the expert has pointed to in the publication are the only ones which relate to the lawsuit. After the expert has isolated each and every part of a publication which relates to the precise issue in the lawsuit, the examiner should ask the expert to link each such passage to the issues in the case.

The examiner should go through this avenue of questioning in excruciating detail for the first couple of passages. By doing so, the examiner signals to the expert that every subsequent publication or activity which the expert claims is related to the precise issues in the case will be met with the same vigorous analysis. The expert accordingly will be extremely cautious about

DEPOSITIONS: Procedures, Strategy and Techniques, designed for use in CLE programs, is the textual abridgement of the looseleaf edition which includes forms on disk. The section and form numbering from the looseleaf edition have been retained in the Professional Education Edition.

making general statements about his or her credentials for the remainder of the deposition. Indeed, the expert may be quick to testify that such credentials are unrelated to the issues in the case merely to speed the deposition along or to avoid the painful scrutiny which has just taken place. As a consequence, the expert effectively will *reduce* his or her own credentials to offer an opinion in the case. When this process is completed, the examiner may find that very little of the expert's once overwhelming curriculum vitae indicates any skill which would permit the expert to offer an opinion in *this* case.

6. Explore the nature and terms of the expert's engagement.

The terms of an expert's engagement are freely discoverable. Indeed Federal Rule 26(a)(2) mandates that those terms be disclosed. The expert's deposition thus can and should include questioning on the nature of the engagement. The questioning, however, must be pointed.

Too often, the examiner, more out of curiosity than anything else, will ask the expert's hourly rate, and then leave the subject altogether. If constructed carefully, questions regarding the terms of the expert's engagement can produce answers which reflect subtle, but palpable, biases. Of course, no expert gets paid on a contingent basis. But, it is equally true that testifying experts sponsored by an adversary are hired by that adversary and are paid by that adversary. In reality, experts are not hired unless they will provide an opinion favorable to the hiring party. Experts know this common sense fact. When a prospective expert is initially contacted by a party's attorney, therefore, that attorney invariably will feel out the expert for the expert's opinion. Often, the attorney first will send to the expert some basic materials about the case such as the complaint, and then ask the expert by telephone or in person whether the expert would be willing to offer an opinion in the case. Even if the attorney does not ask the expert to offer a supporting opinion, the expert knows which

DEPOSITIONS: Procedures, Strategy and Techniques, designed for use in CLE programs, is the textual abridgement of the looseleaf edition which includes forms on disk. The section and form numbering from the looseleaf edition have been retained in the Professional Education Edition.

side the attorney is on. If the expert agrees to offer an opinion in the case, the expert has an expectation of being paid a healthy hourly rate. If, on the other hand, the expert declines the engagement, the expert will not be paid. In other words, in virtually every case, the expert has a financial incentive to offer an opinion favorable to the party which contacts and sponsors that expert. That incentive will not be ignored by the jury.

In order to establish this financial incentive, the examining attorney should ask the expert deponent to provide a step-by-step chronology of the initial contacts and communications between the hiring attorney and that expert. The following avenues of inquiry may prove effective:

(1) When were you first contacted in connection with this case? Who contacted you? By phone or other? Prior to the time when you were first contacted in this case, you had no understanding of the facts or legal issues?

(2) When [name of the lawyer] contacted you, did he or she indicate his or her role in the case? Whom he or she represented?

(3) What else did the lawyer say to you during that initial contact? What did you say to the lawyer?

(4) Did you have an understanding as to who referred the lawyer to you? Relationship between the expert and the referral source?

(5) Did you agree to provide a supportive opinion before or after you discussed the financial terms of your engagement with counsel? If before, the sponsoring attorney agreed to pay the expert the expert's hourly rate only after that attorney learned of the favorable opinion. If the expert arrived at the favorable opinion only after the sponsoring attorney agreed to pay the hourly rate, then the expert can be led to admit that he or she understood the financial incentives involved before reaching the favorable opinion.

DEPOSITIONS: Procedures, Strategy and Techniques, designed for use in CLE programs, is the textual abridgement of the looseleaf edition which includes forms on disk. The section and form numbering from the looseleaf edition have been retained in the Professional Education Edition.

The examiner also should inquire as to the nature of the working relationship between the expert and the sponsoring attorney. The expert learns about the case from the sponsoring attorney. In initial oral conversations with the sponsoring attorney, the expert usually obtains the facts of the case from that attorney's point of view. Apart from those conversations, the expert typically learns about the case from documents selected and delivered by the sponsoring attorney. The expert, therefore, may not have seen any unfavorable evidence at all, or may have seen such evidence only after arriving at an opinion.

Moreover, experts often receive additional material from their sponsoring lawyers in the period between issuing their opinion and their deposition. Sponsoring lawyers sometimes race to get an opinion on file, and then worry about supporting that opinion later in litigation. Experts, prodded by their sponsoring attorneys, may do the same.

The examiner should exploit this routine by asking the expert what information the expert reviewed *before* arriving at the opinion. If this inquiry is conducted skillfully, the expert may acknowledge that the opinion was formed before the expert had access to key countervailing documents or information. The examiner should establish the initial date of the engagement and the date on which the expert arrived at the opinion. The examiner should then attempt to establish that the information which was made available to the expert before the opinion was formed was not complete. The examiner may wish to compare the documents on which the expert relied in preparing for the deposition with the documents which the expert relied upon in forming the opinion. Where the expert's deposition follows the submission of the expert's opinion by weeks or months, the expert often will be given additional supporting or refuting information to help the expert in the deposition. That later-supplied information may not have been considered by the expert in arriving at the initial opinion.

DEPOSITIONS: Procedures, Strategy and Techniques, designed for use in CLE programs, is the textual abridgement of the looseleaf edition which includes forms on disk. The section and form numbering from the looseleaf edition have been retained in the Professional Education Edition.

7. Identify the case-specific information which the expert has reviewed in reaching an opinion, and in preparing for the deposition.

In the course of developing the chronology of the expert's contacts with the sponsoring attorney, the identity of the case-specific information which the expert has reviewed in reaching an opinion and in preparing for the deposition may be revealed. If not, the examiner must obtain a precise catalogue from the expert of each and every piece of case-specific information relied upon by that expert. There is no dispute that the expert must disclose all such materials.

Experts often bring their "file" with them to the deposition and refer vaguely to their "file" when asked about the information on which they relied in forming their opinions. The examiner must force the expert to identify each item in that file for the record. The examiner should then establish that the catalogue of items is complete—that the expert relied only on these case-specific materials (and perhaps oral communications with the sponsoring attorney and party) and no others. Once the catalogue of information is established, the examiner should examine the expert with respect to each item. The questioning again must be focused on linking the information in each identified item with the expert's opinion: What line or lines of a document were relied upon in reaching the opinion?

8. Identify the persons with whom the expert has discussed the case, including representatives of the client and assistants.

Experts rely upon others in formulating their opinions. They obtain information from their sponsoring attorneys. They also gain insight from communications with the sponsoring party or its representatives. Those communications can be a rich subject of deposition questioning. If the expert has relied upon communications with the sponsoring party, the expert must disclose that reliance. Where the communications involve persons

---

DEPOSITIONS: Procedures, Strategy and Techniques, designed for use in CLE programs, is the textual abridgement of the looseleaf edition which includes forms on disk. The section and form numbering from the looseleaf edition have been retained in the Professional Education Edition.

outside the parameters of the attorney-client privilege or the work-product doctrine, the expert must disclose their exact content. At a minimum, the expert can be led to concede that all of the information on which the expert relies has been received or filtered by the sponsoring party or the sponsoring party's counsel.

The examiner also should determine which portions of the expert's opinion have been prepared by persons other than that expert. In some cases, the party may supply a part of the expert's written report. More commonly, the expert will rely upon associates or re-search assistants for information and drafting of various parts of a written opinion. The examiner must define those portions of the expert's opinion which have been prepared by someone other than the expert. Such asso-ciates generally would not themselves be qualified to render an expert opinion in the case. Moreover, testify-ing experts who rely heavily on work prepared by their associates or subordinates do not always know enough about that work to defend it at the deposition, or at trial.

9. Crystalize and exhaust the expert's opinions in the case.

If the examiner accomplishes nothing else at the expert's deposition, he or she must at least lock the expert in to clear and complete opinions. There is no reason to avoid asking the expert these basic questions: (1) Do you have any opinions in this case? (2) What are those opinions? (3) Apart from these opinions, are there any other opinions which you have in this case? (4) Have you given us an exhaustive list of your opinions in this case? (5) Have you been asked to provide any additional opinions in this case? (6) Do you intend to provide any additional opinions in this case? (7) Do you intend to perform any additional expert services in this case? (8) What is the nature of these services? (9) Are the opinions which you have expressed in this deposition complete?

DEPOSITIONS: Procedures, Strategy and Techniques, designed for use in CLE programs, is the textual abridgement of the looseleaf edition which includes forms on disk. The section and form numbering from the looseleaf edition have been retained in the Professional Education Edition.

The expert should indicate that the opinions which have been stated at the deposition are complete and exhaustive. If the expert indicates an intent to change or supplement the opinions, the examiner must establish the nature of the changes and additions. The examiner should then be sure to leave the deposition open for further questioning when the new opinions are provided, and should pursue appropriate court sanctions, if justified.

§ 15.5 Defending the Expert Deposition

When a party decides to call an expert witness at trial to support its case, that party takes on a risk. Theoretically, the expert is not a party and cannot make binding admissions. As a practical matter, however, the fact-finder will align the expert with the sponsoring party. Accordingly, if the expert offers nonsupportive opinions or ever fails to offer promised supporting opinions, that expert can seriously harm a party's case.

A central testing point for the strength of an expert's testimony is the expert's deposition. Apart from carefully selecting a testifying expert, the party, therefore, must work closely with the expert before, during and after the expert's deposition. This process is complicated by the fact that, for purposes of the attorney-client and work-product privileges, the expert is *not* treated as a party. While communications between an attorney and client cannot be discovered, and while the materials prepared by attorneys and their agents for litigation generally are protected from discovery, materials prepared by an expert—even in consultation with an attorney—will not necessarily be immune from discovery. Indeed, experts will be required to disclose all work-papers, all prior drafts of their reports and all materials on which they relied in preparing their opinion. *See, e.g.,* Fed.R.Civ.P. 26(a)(2). If an attorney's memorandum is in the possession of an expert, that memorandum may be turned over to the adversary in discovery.

DEPOSITIONS: Procedures, Strategy and Techniques, designed for use in CLE programs, is the textual abridgement of the looseleaf edition which includes forms on disk. The section and form numbering from the looseleaf edition have been retained in the Professional Education Edition.

Notes

The preparation of an expert for deposition and trial testimony thus presents the attorney with a tremendous challenge. Because the expert's testimony is vital to a party's case, the attorney must prepare the expert. In preparing the expert, however, the attorney must be sensitive to the risk that materials and communications used in the course of that preparation may be disclosed to the adversary. The most effective way to prepare an expert, therefore, is to treat the expert as a party witness, but to insure that the expert receive nothing from the attorney which the attorney has not already disclosed to the adversary or which the attorney would not be afraid to disclose to the adversary. Within this general approach to defending an expert witness, attorneys should also consider the following tactical guidelines:

1. Select an expert knowing the expert's weaknesses.

The most important step in employing an expert witness is selection. The expert, of course, must have "specialized knowledge" regarding the subject matter of the litigation. Typically, the attorney will be able to find several potential experts with impressive credentials in fields related to the litigation. The challenge is to identify the strengths and weaknesses of each of the potential witnesses.

First, beyond "specialized knowledge," the expert must be qualified to offer an opinion regarding the precise issues which are at stake in the litigation. The attorney should ask the expert to state how the expert's qualifications directly relate to the issues on which the expert will opine. If the expert cannot directly trace his or her qualifications to the narrow issues in the case, the attorney should then determine whether the expert, after preparation, will be able to offer credible opinions on those precise issues. If the attorney determines that the expert, even after preparation, will not be able to offer a credible precise opinion, the attorney should consider trying to find another expert.

DEPOSITIONS: Procedures, Strategy and Techniques, designed for use in CLE programs, is the textual abridgement of the looseleaf edition which includes forms on disk. The section and form numbering from the looseleaf edition have been retained in the Professional Education Edition.

Second, the attorney should determine whether the expert is a professional witness, an academic or both. A professional witness is a witness employed by a litigation consulting firm whose primary job is to offer expert trial testimony. Such an expert has the advantage of experience with the judicial process, including experience under cross-examination. The expert will develop and deliver an opinion with a thorough understanding of the adversary system. The professional expert will understand, therefore, the need to be firm in the delivery of an opinion, and the need to resist making concessions under rigorous cross-examination. Moreover, the professional expert will likely understand the sensitivity of the materials relied upon in developing an opinion. Professional consulting firms, for example, typically have document retention policies by which experts are directed to discard all prior drafts of their reports.

Professional experts come with some disadvantages as well. They are expensive. They may have a relative lack of credibility based on their status as professional witnesses. Such witnesses also are part of large professional consulting firms in which other persons in the firm may do the great majority of the preparation work. This organizational structure not only results in duplication of effort and higher fees; it also results in a witness who may not have a firm grasp of the underlying basis of an opinion.

Academic experts come with the reverse strengths and weaknesses. They tend to be credible witnesses because their testimony grows out of their life's work and research. They usually do their own preparatory work and that work is usually thorough. They tend to be less expensive than their professional counterparts.

Academic witnesses, however, tend to have little litigation experience. They are credible to a fault. Their opinions are malleable. Those opinions may conform to the witness' academic position rather than to a party's litigation position. When push comes to shove (*i.e.* under deposition examination), the academic expert

DEPOSITIONS: Procedures, Strategy and Techniques, designed for use in CLE programs, is the textual abridgement of the looseleaf edition which includes forms on disk. The section and form numbering from the looseleaf edition have been retained in the Professional Education Edition.

207

may abandon a litigation position before abandoning a doctrinal academic position. The academic witness often will have a wealth of published material which sets out that doctrinal position. The examiner, therefore, will have a rich source of material from which to push the expert to the boundaries of any litigation position. In light of these advantages and disadvantages for academic and professional witnesses, the "best" expert witness is an academic who has significant litigation experience, who has written or said nothing that will be harmful to the party, who is prepared to work hard, and who has "specialized knowledge" of the precise issues in the case.

2. Be careful during the initial contacts with an expert witness.

Attorneys should assume that their initial communications with an expert will be discoverable. Attorneys thus should not create any perception of bias during these contacts. They must avoid that perception while informing the expert of the key facts and issues in the case. One way to accomplish this difficult task is to follow these steps:

1. Attorneys should introduce themselves and indicate their position in the litigation.

2. Attorneys should ask potential expert witnesses whether they feel qualified to offer an opinion on the issues in the case.

3. The issues should be stated as objectively as possible.

4. If the witness states that he or she would be qualified to offer an opinion on the issues in the case, the attorney should follow up by asking for those qualifications and for the expert's usual rate.

5. The attorney should then ask to meet the witness *face-to-face*.

DEPOSITIONS: Procedures, Strategy and Techniques, designed for use in CLE programs, is the textual abridgement of the looseleaf edition which includes forms on disk. The section and form numbering from the looseleaf edition have been retained in the Professional Education Edition.

3. Give experts all relevant material before they complete their opinions.

As early as possible after the attorney decides to employ the expert, the attorney should give to the expert a complete file of materials in the case, including the pleadings and the significant evidence produced by discovery. The file should contain both "good" and "bad" evidence for the party's case. Experts must be able to testify that they have reviewed *all* of the relevant material in the case *before* reaching their opinions. If new material comes to light after an expert has completed a report or given opinion testimony, the expert must be informed of that new material. The expert should then be prepared to incorporate or to account for that material in developing a complete opinion.

4. Make sure that the expert understands the facts.

If an expert is not given all relevant factual material, the expert will not be fully prepared to testify. The adversary can use the expert's lack of particularized knowledge of the facts and documents in the case to frame hypothetical questions based on those facts and documents. Unless the expert has some awareness of the nature and bases of these hypothetical questions, the expert may offer harmful concessions.

After thorough preparation, an expert can actually become more familiar with the facts of the case than the examining attorney. If the expert has a keen understanding of the facts, that expert cannot easily be led to offer damaging concessions in the deposition. When that keen factual understanding is coupled with an expert's specialized knowledge, the expert becomes difficult to dissect.

Moreover, when an expert is well-versed in the facts of the case, the expert's deposition and trial testimony can become an effective summation of the facts supporting the sponsoring party's case. Hence, when examining attorneys ask an expert—as they invariably do—for the

DEPOSITIONS: Procedures, Strategy and Techniques, designed for use in CLE programs, is the textual abridgement of the looseleaf edition which includes forms on disk. The section and form numbering from the looseleaf edition have been retained in the Professional Education Edition.

bases of the expert's opinion, the expert can wax poetic about the key facts in the case. The expert need not supply any citations for those facts. Nor do the bases for those facts themselves have to be admissible at trial. Rather, the expert can testify based upon a general memory of the "record" in the case. For example, the expert may credibly state that the opinion is based on his or her understanding of testimony adduced at the adversary's deposition. If the expert in fact has reviewed materials such as the adversary's deposition transcript, the expert can offer a vigorous factual defense of the sponsoring party's case while providing an opinion on the ultimate issues. It is essential, therefore, that the attorney sponsoring and defending the expert provide that expert with the relevant facts and evidentiary materials in the case.

5. Make the expert aware of litigation tactics.

Some experts will have no prior exposure to litigation. Others, particularly those from expert consulting firms, may have substantial litigation experience. All experts should be taught or reminded that the litigation process is an adversarial one. The deposition is not a classroom, a lecture hall or even a professional seminar. The examining attorney is not a disinterested listener, or even an engaged audience member. Appearances notwithstanding, the examiner is not the expert's friend. Nor is the examiner really awestruck by the expert's credentials.

For an expert used to friendly audiences, the deposition process will be quite foreign. The expert must be informed that the goal of the examining attorney is to obtain damaging concessions from the expert. Questions are not asked out of intellectual curiosity; rather, they are designed to elicit a particular response. Accordingly, experts—perhaps even more than lay witnesses—should be taught to answer only the questions asked and to measure their responses.

DEPOSITIONS: Procedures, Strategy and Techniques, designed for use in CLE programs, is the textual abridgement of the looseleaf edition which includes forms on disk. The section and form numbering from the looseleaf edition have been retained in the Professional Education Edition.

6.   Allow the expert to be an expert.

While the preparatory techniques used for lay witnesses should be applied to experts, the defending attorney should not lose sight of the expert's unique value to the case.   Certainly the expert must be made aware of the adversarial nature of the litigation process and of the risk of volunteering information not directly responsive to questions.

But there is a danger that an expert may be too inhibited at the deposition.   The expert must display profound confidence in the opinions and their bases. Thus, the expert should not be reticent about those opinions and the degree of support for them.   An expert witness can use the deposition format to advertise the strength of the case to the opponent.   Indeed, a particularly strong expert deposition can induce attractive settlement offers.

The defending attorney therefore should encourage the expert to testify fully and even persuasively about the expert's opinions and the wealth of their theoretical and factual support, without volunteering harmful information to the adversary.   This difficult preparatory job can be accomplished if the defending attorney requires the expert to rehearse a full and compelling presentation of the expert's opinions in advance of the deposition. The expert should be asked to respond orally to the following questions in advance of the deposition:

1.   What are your opinions with respect to this litigation?

2.   What is the theoretical and factual support for each of those opinions?

The expert's initial oral response to these questions will be clumsy and incomplete.   But as the expert becomes comfortable with the process, the opinions will become more artful and the support more complete. During this process, the defending attorney should remind the expert of additional factual support for the opinions.   In addition, the defending attorney should ask the expert how he or she might accommodate facts

---

DEPOSITIONS: Procedures, Strategy and Techniques, designed for use in CLE programs, is the textual abridgement of the looseleaf edition which includes forms on disk.   The section and form numbering from the looseleaf edition have been retained in the Professional Education Edition.

which appear to be contrary to the opinion. Ultimately, the expert will be able to deliver clear and compelling opinions on ultimate issues with strong factual foundation.

If this preparation is done properly, the expert can be encouraged to be forthcoming in the deposition about the expert's opinions and their bases. The expert will in fact advertise the case. At the same time, the expert can be warned not to volunteer information in response to any question which does not directly seek the expert's prepared opinions and their bases.

DEPOSITIONS: Procedures, Strategy and Techniques, designed for use in CLE programs, is the textual abridgement of the looseleaf edition which includes forms on disk. The section and form numbering from the looseleaf edition have been retained in the Professional Education Edition.

Part IV

USE OF DEPOSITION AT TRIAL

Chapter 17

USING THE DEPOSITION AT TRIAL

Table of Sections

---

§ 17.1 Introduction

The distinction between depositions used for discovery and those used for evidence at trial becomes acute when the examiner begins contemplating the introduction of deposition testimony into evidence. The scope of discovery is expressly broader than the scope of admissible testimony. Deposition questions need be only reasonably calculated to lead to admissible evidence; they need not produce admissible evidence. An answer helpful in discovery may well be inadmissible in evidence at trial. In order to avoid producing a deposition transcript which is unuseable at trial, the examiner should of course read the relevant rules of evidence in conjunction with this and the preceding chapter before even taking the deposition. Then, in preparing to use deposition

---

DEPOSITIONS: Procedures, Strategy and Techniques, designed for use in CLE programs, is the textual abridgement of the looseleaf edition which includes forms on disk. The section and form numbering from the looseleaf edition have been retained in the Professional Education Edition.

testimony at trial, the examiner should return to this chapter and to Forms 17–1 thru 17–8 with the singular goal of extracting admissible evidence.

§ 17.2 Rules Governing the Use of Depositions at Trial

The rules of procedure and of evidence both govern the admissibility at trial of deposition testimony. Federal Rule of Civil Procedure 32(a) allows the use at trial of any part of a deposition against any party who received reasonable notice of the deposition. Objections to notice are waived either by attendance of the party or its representative at the deposition (Fed.R.Civ.P. 32(a)), or by failure to serve prompt written objection to the notice upon the party providing the notice. Fed.R.Civ.P. 32(d)(1).

The discovery rules, however, limit the general purposes for which a deposition can be used. The deposition of a party or an unavailable witness can be used for "any purpose." Fed.R.Civ.P. 32(a)(2), (3). But the deposition of an available, non-party witness can only be used, (1) to contradict the witness's trial testimony, (2) to impeach the witness, or (3) for any other purposes permitted by the federal rules of evidence. Fed.R.Civ.P. 32(a)(1). These discovery rules must be satisfied before a deposition can be used at trial.

Even if those discovery rules are satisfied, however, the introducing party must overcome a second obstacle. Each question and answer of deposition testimony must also be admissible under the rules of evidence, which are applied as if the deponent were testifying live at trial. Deposition testimony, therefore, can be used at trial only if the rules of procedure and of evidence are both satisfied.

§ 17.3 Use of Adverse Party's Deposition at Trial

The deposition of an adverse party generally can be used at trial for "any purpose." Fed.R.Civ.P. 32(a)(2). The only narrow exceptions to this rule are for parties

DEPOSITIONS: Procedures, Strategy and Techniques, designed for use in CLE programs, is the textual abridgement of the looseleaf edition which includes forms on disk. The section and form numbering from the looseleaf edition have been retained in the Professional Education Edition.

who, despite due diligence, were unable to obtain counsel to represent them at their deposition, or who attended their depositions while a timely-filed motion for protective order was pending.

Included within the definition of adverse "party" are:

(1) officer of a party at the time of the deposition;

(2) director of a party at the time of the deposition;

(3) managing agent of a party at the time of the deposition; and

(4) any person designated by an organizational party to testify on its behalf.

Although some courts have stretched this rule to include within the definition of "adverse party" all deponents whose interests are "adverse" to the offeror, *see e.g.* Coughlin v. Capitol Cement Co., 571 F.2d 290, 308 (5th Cir.1978) (applying "any purpose" standard to available, non-party whom the court presumed to be adverse to offeror), the rule is limited to deponents who are *both* parties and adverse to the offering party. There is no doubt, however, that the deposition of an individual who qualifies as an adverse party can, under the discovery rules, be used for any purpose, even when the deponent is available to testify at trial. *See e.g.,* Fey v. Walston & Co., Inc., 493 F.2d 1036 (7th Cir.1974). The deposing party, using Form 17–2, can plan to use the deposition of such an adverse party, therefore, at trial for any purpose, including as substantive evidence. However, the offering party must also be certain that each portion of the testimony be admissible under the rules of evidence as if the deponent's testimony were being given live.

§ 17.4 Use of Unavailable Witness's Deposition at Trial

The deposition of a party or a non-party who is unavailable at trial may also be used at trial for "any purpose," including as substantive evidence. *See e.g.*

DEPOSITIONS: Procedures, Strategy and Techniques, designed for use in CLE programs, is the textual abridgement of the looseleaf edition which includes forms on disk. The section and form numbering from the looseleaf edition have been retained in the Professional Education Edition.

Fed.R.Civ.P. 32(a)(3); Form 17–3. The unavailability of the witness is determined by the court as of the time the testimony is offered at trial. *See e.g.* United States v. IBM Corp., 90 F.R.D. 377 (S.D.N.Y.1981). A witness is unavailable within the meaning of the rule if the court finds that at the time his testimony is offered at trial, he is:

(1) Dead.

(2)(a) More than 100 miles from the place of trial, measured as-the-crow-flies, *see e.g.* SCM Corp. v. Xerox Corp., 76 F.R.D. 214 (D.Conn.1977), and in accordance with judicial notice. Ikerd v. Lapworth, 435 F.2d 197 (7th Cir.1970), or

(b) outside of the United States.

If, however, the witness's absence was affirmatively caused by the offering party, the deposition will not be admissible as substantive evidence.

(3) Unable to attend or testify because of age, illness, infirmity or imprisonment, or

(4) Unable to be compelled to testify by subpoena.

In addition, regardless of the unavailability of the deponent under these rules, the court has authority to allow the deposition to be used where the offering party has, with proper notice, moved and shown that "exceptional circumstances" exist which make it desirable to introduce the deposition itself into evidence. Fed. R.Civ.P. 32(a)(3).

In ruling on the motion to allow such deposition testimony, however, the court must give due regard to the policy of presenting live, oral testimony in court wherever possible. *Id.* While rare, rulings that "exceptional circumstances" exist can arise where the necessity of a witness's testimony becomes apparent to counsel in the middle of trial and the court decides not to grant a continuance to allow the procurement of the witness. *See e.g.* Huff v. Marine Tank Testing Corp., 631 F.2d 1140 (4th Cir.1980). Thus, where the court finds exceptional circumstances or where the deponent is otherwise unavailable to provide live testimony, a deposition can be used for "any purpose," provided that the testimony is admissible under the rules of evidence.

§ 17.5 Use of Available, Non-party Depositions at Trial

Federal Rule of Civil Procedure 32(a)(1), in keeping with the policy favoring the presentation of live testimony at trial, limits the use of the deposition testimony of non-parties who are available at trial:

> Any deposition may be used by any party for the purpose of contradicting or impeaching the testimony of deponent as a witness, or for any other purposes permitted by the Federal Rules of Evidence.

When the deposition is used to contradict testimony or to impeach a witness, it is not admitted as substantive evidence. Rather, the deposition transcript of a deponent can be used merely to attack the testimony or credibility of that deponent when he offers live testimony at trial. Inconsistencies within the deposition itself thus cannot be used to "impeach" the deponent unless the deponent testifies at trial. *See* Rogers v. Roth, 477 F.2d 1154 (10th Cir.1973).

The deposition of an available, non-party witness may also be used for any purpose permitted by the federal rules of evidence. Those rules expand the possible uses for deposition testimony by permitting:

(1) The use of a deposition to impeach one's own witness, where the witness offers live testimony, Fed.R.Evid. 607;

(2) The use of a deposition to refresh a live witness' recollection. Fed.R.Evid. 612, 803(5); and

(3) The use of a deposition as a prior statement of the witness which need not be shown to the witness. Fed.R.Evid. 613(a).

DEPOSITIONS: Procedures, Strategy and Techniques, designed for use in CLE programs, is the textual abridgement of the looseleaf edition which includes forms on disk. The section and form numbering from the looseleaf edition have been retained in the Professional Education Edition.

More significantly, however, the federal rules of evidence allow use of an available, non-party deposition as *substantive evidence* where:

(1) The deposition testimony is inconsistent with the deponent's live testimony, or is consistent with the deponent's live testimony but is offered to refute an allegation of inconsistency, Fed. R.Evid. 801(1);

(2) The deposition testimony is a statement by any employee of a party (not just an officer, director, managing agent or designated representative) and is offered as an admission of a party opponent. Fed.R.Evid. 801(d)(2); or

(3) The deposition testimony has sufficient "circumstantial guarantees of trustworthiness" so as to allow its introduction into evidence. Fed. R.Civ.P. 803(24).

Form 17–4 sets forth these various uses at trial of the depositions of an available, non-party witness.

§ 17.6 Party's Use of Own Deposition

A party may use his own deposition at trial to contradict or impeach his own trial testimony, as permitted under the federal rules of evidence. *See* Fed.R.Evid. 607; Form 17–5. In addition, a party may introduce into substantive evidence his prior deposition testimony where that testimony is offered to rebut a claim that his trial testimony is the product of recent fabrication or improper influence or motive. Fed.R.Evid. 801(1)(B).

Otherwise, however, a party may use his own deposition at trial as substantive evidence only if he is "unavailable." In this context, "unavailability" is narrowly defined. If the party is dead or infirm at the time of the deposition, courts allow the introduction into evidence of a prior deposition. *See e.g.* Treharne v. Callahan, 426 F.2d 58 (3d Cir.1970). Moreover, the majority rule allows a party who at the time of trial is more than 100 miles from the courthouse to introduce

DEPOSITIONS: Procedures, Strategy and Techniques, designed for use in CLE programs, is the textual abridgement of the looseleaf edition which includes forms on disk. The section and form numbering from the looseleaf edition have been retained in the Professional Education Edition.

his own deposition into evidence. *See* Richmond v. Brooks, 227 F.2d 490 (2d Cir.1955). Although this rule permits a party to "procure" his own unavailability, the courts have reasoned that because the rule makes no distinction between parties and non-parties (Fed. R.Civ.P. 32(a)(3)), parties are free to choose not to appear live at trial. *Id.*

§ 17.7 Use of Deposition From Prior Action

Depositions taken in federal or state court actions can be used in subsequent federal actions under limited circumstances. First, the original deposition must have been properly filed. Second, the deposition must have been lawfully taken, under the rules governing the jurisdiction in which the original action was filed. Third, the subsequent federal action must involve the same "subject matter" as the original action. Fourth, the subsequent action must involve the same parties as the original action, or at least their representatives or successors in interest. Fed.R.Civ.P. 32(a)(4). *See also* Form 17–6. The deposition can be used even if the action in which it was taken has not been dismissed.

The federal discovery rules, however, also permit the use of prior depositions in any other manner sanctioned by the federal rules of evidence. Under those rules, if the deponent is unavailable to testify in the current proceeding, his prior deposition testimony can be introduced into evidence if that testimony was lawfully taken and if the party against whom that testimony is currently being offered (or a predecessor in interest) had a full and fair opportunity to examine the deponent. Fed.R.Evid. 804(b)(1). The party currently offering the examination into evidence need not have been a party to the initial proceedings. Nor, under the rules of evidence, need the subject matters of the two actions be similar, so long as the party against whom the deposition is currently offered had a fair opportunity to examine the deponent.

DEPOSITIONS: Procedures, Strategy and Techniques, designed for use in CLE programs, is the textual abridgement of the looseleaf edition which includes forms on disk. The section and form numbering from the looseleaf edition have been retained in the Professional Education Edition.

§ 17.8 Limits on the Use of Depositions at Trial Under the Rules of Evidence

A deposition cannot be used at trial for any purpose unless the portions offered are "admissible under the rules of evidence applied as though the witness were there and testifying." Fed.R.Civ.P. 32(a). Hence, the offering party must ensure that:

(1) the testimony is relevant, Fed.R.Evid. 401;

(2) the testimony's probative value outweighs its prejudicial impact, Fed.R.Evid. 403;

(3) the testimony is not redundant, cumulative, confusing or a waste of time, Fed.R.Evid. 403;

(4) the testimony is a proper method of establishing character, where appropriate, Fed.R.Evid. 404;

(5) the testimony does not run afoul of any exclusion based on public policy, such as subsequent remedial measures, Fed.R.Evid. 407–412;

(6) the testimony is not subject to any available privilege, Fed.R.Evid. 501;

(7) the witness is competent to testify as to the offered matters, Fed.R.Evid. 601–607, 701–706;

(8) the method of interrogation (i.e. leading questions) was proper, Fed.R.Evid. 611; and

(9) the testimony is not otherwise inadmissible as hearsay. Fed.R.Evid. 801–805.

In addition, the party designating the deposition transcript must remember the rule of "completeness." Portions of deposition testimony will be admitted only in their proper context. Deposition testimony, therefore, must be offered together with all portions necessary to correct any misimpression created by reading that testimony out of context. Fed.R.Civ.P. 32(d)(4).

Form 17–7 provides a checklist of the possible evidentiary objections.

DEPOSITIONS: Procedures, Strategy and Techniques, designed for use in CLE programs, is the textual abridgement of the looseleaf edition which includes forms on disk. The section and form numbering from the looseleaf edition have been retained in the Professional Education Edition.

§ 17.9 Objections to Admissibility of Deposition Testimony at Trial

Any objection to the admissibility of deposition testimony not waived may be made at trial. Fed.R.Civ.P. 32(b). Objections to deposition notice, to the qualifications of the officer, to the oath, to the completion of the deposition record and to the form of written deposition questions are waived if they are not made promptly. *See* Fed.R.Civ.P. 32(d)(1), (2), (3), (4).

More importantly, objections as to the admissibility of evidence at trial can be waived if the objection goes to the form of the deposition question or if the basis for the objection could have been removed if it had been raised at the deposition. Fed.R.Civ.P. 32(d)(3)(A). As a general rule, these objections do not involve the substance of the testimony. In fact, the rules create a presumption that objections to the competency of the witness and the relevance of the testimony are not waived by the failure to make them at deposition. Fed.R.Civ.P. 32(d)(3)(A). The presumption is rebutted only upon a difficult showing that such objections could have been cured if raised at deposition. Form 17–8 is a worksheet which enables the attorney to organize the possible objections to the admissibility of deposition testimony at trial.

*

DEPOSITIONS: Procedures, Strategy and Techniques, designed for use in CLE programs, is the textual abridgement of the looseleaf edition which includes forms on disk. The section and form numbering from the looseleaf edition have been retained in the Professional Education Edition.

Appendix

DEPOSITION RULES IN EACH STATE

FEDERAL
RULE 26(b)(1)
Para. 1

(b) **Discovery Scope and Limits.** Unless otherwise limited by order of the court in accordance with these rules, the scope of discovery is as follows:—

(1) In General. Parties may obtain discovery regarding any matter, *not privileged* (emphasis added), which is relevant to the subject matter involved in the pending action, whether it relates to the claim or defense of the party seeking discovery or to the claim or defense of any other party, including the existence, description, nature, custody, condition and location of any books, documents, or other tangible things and the identity and location of persons having knowledge of any discoverable matter. The information sought need not be admissible at the trial if the information sought appears reasonably calculated to lead to the discovery of admissible evidence.

ALABAMA
RULE 26(b)(1)

Mirrors Federal Rule 26(b)(1), Para. 1

ALASKA
RULE 26(b)(1)

Mirrors Federal Rule 26(b)(1), Para. 1

ARIZONA
RULE 26(b)(1)

Mirrors Federal Rule 26(b)(1), Para. 1

ARKANSAS
RULE 26(b)(1)

Substantially similar to Federal Rule 26(b)(1), Para. 1. Subsection substitutes "issues" for "subject matter involved." It omits the location of "any books, documents, or other tangible things," and instead focuses on the location of persons who have knowledge of any discoverable matter *or who will or may be*

223

called as a witness at the trial of any cause *(emphasis added).*

CALIFORNIA
SECTION 2016(b)

Substantially similar to Federal Rule 26(b)(1), Para. 1. Scope of examination is subject to subdivision (b) or (d) of Section 2019 of this code. Subsection (b) has also added that, "All matters which are privileged against disclosure upon the trial under the law of this state are privileged against disclosure through any discovery procedure. This article shall not be construed to change the law of this state with respect to the existence of any privilege, whether provided for by statute or by judicial decision."

SECTION 2023(a)(1)

Misuses of the discovery process include, but are not limited to, the following: (1) Persisting, over objection and without substantial justification, in an attempt to obtain information or materials that are outside the scope of permissible discovery.

SECTION 2025(a)

Any party may obtain discovery within the scope delimited by Section 2017, and subject to the restrictions set forth in Section 2019, by taking in California the oral deposition of any person, including any party to the action.

COLORADO
RULE 26(b)(1)

Mirrors Federal Rule 26(b)(1), Para. 1

CONNECTICUT
SECTION 218

Scope of Discovery—In General. In any civil action, in any probate appeal, or in any administrative appeal where the court finds it reasonably probable that evidence outside the record will be required, a party may obtain in accordance with the provisions of this chapter discovery of information or disclosure, production and inspection of papers, books or document material to the subject matter involved in the pending action, which are *not privileged* (emphasis added), whether the discovery or disclosure relates to the claim or defense of the party seeking discovery or to the claim or defense of any other party, and which are within the knowledge, possession or power of the party or person to whom the discovery is addressed. Discovery shall be permitted if the disclosure sought would be of assistance in the prosecution or defense of the action and if it can be provided by the disclosing party or person with substantially greater facility than it could otherwise be obtained by the party seeking disclosure. It shall not be ground for objection that the information sought will be inadmissible at trial if the information sought appears reasonably calculated to lead to the discovery of admissible evidence. Written opinions of health care providers concerning evidence of medical negligence as provided by Section 12 of P.A. 86–338 shall not be subject to discovery except as provided in that section.

SECTION 219

Scope of Discovery—Materials Prepared in Anticipation of Litigation; Statements of Parties. A party may obtain, without the showing required under this section, discovery of his own statement and of any *non-privileged* (emphasis added) statement of any other party concerning the action or its subject matter.

DELAWARE
RULE 26(b)(1)

Mirrors Federal Rule 26(b)(1), Para. 1

D.C.
RULE 26(b)(1)

Mirrors Federal Rule 26(b)(1), Para. 1

FLORIDA
RULE 1.280(b)(1)

Mirrors Federal Rule 26(b)(1), Para. 1

GEORGIA
SECTION 9–11–26(b)(1)

Mirrors Federal Rule 26(b)(1), Para. 1

HAWAII
RULE 26(b)(1)

Mirrors Federal Rule 26(b)(1), Para. 1

IDAHO
RULE 26(b)(1)

Mirrors Federal Rule 26(b)(1), Para. 1

RULE 26(b)(3)

... In ordering discovery of such materials when the required showing has been made, the court shall protect against disclosure of the mental impressions, conclusions, opinions, or legal theories of an attorney or other representative of a party concerning the litigation, *including communications between the attorney and client, whether written or oral* (emphasis added).

ILLINOIS
SECTION 201(b)(2)

Privilege and Work Product. All matters that are privileged against disclosure on the trial, *including privileged communications between a party or his agent and the attorney for the party, are privileged against disclosure through any discovery procedure* (emphasis added). Material prepared by or for a party in preparation for trial is subject to discovery only if it does not contain or disclose the theories, mental impressions, or litigation plans of the party's attorney. The court may apportion the cost involved in originally securing the discoverable material, including when appropriate a reasonable attorney's fee, in such manner as is just.

SECTION 219(d)

Abuse of Discovery Procedures. ... If a party willfully obtains or attempts to obtain information by an improper discovery method, willfully obtains or attempts to obtain information to which he is not entitled, or otherwise abuses these discovery rules, the court may enter any order provided for in paragraph (c) of this rule.

INDIANA
RULE 26(B)(1)

Mirrors Federal Rule 26(b)(1), Para. 1

IOWA
RULE 122(a)

Mirrors Federal Rule 26(b)(1), Para. 1

KANSAS
SECTION 60–226(b)(1)

Mirrors Federal Rule 26(b)(1) except for addition of sentence: "Except as permitted under paragraph (3) of this subsection, a party shall not require a deponent to produce, or submit for inspection, any writing prepared by, or under the supervision of, an attorney in preparation for trial."

KENTUCKY
RULE 26.02(1)

Mirrors Federal Rule 26(b)(1), Para. 1

LOUISIANA
ARTICLE 1422

Mirrors Federal Rule 26(b)(1), Para. 1

MAINE
RULE 26(b)(1)

Mirrors Federal Rule 26(b)(1), Para. 1

MARYLAND
RULE 2–402(a)

Substantially similar to Federal Rule 26(b)(1), Para. 1. Subsection adds that "it is not ground for objection that the information sought *is already known to or otherwise obtainable by the party seeking discovery* (emphasis added) or that the information will be inadmissible at the trial if the information sought appears reasonably calculated to lead to the discovery of admissible evidence." It also adds, "An interrogatory or deposition question otherwise proper is not objectionable merely because the response involves an opinion or contention that relates to fact or the application of law to fact."

MASSACHUSETTS
RULE 26(b)(1)

Mirrors Federal Rule 26(b)(1), Para. 1

MICHIGAN
RULE 2.302(B)(1)(a)

Mirrors Federal Rule 26(b)(1), Para. 1

RULE 2.302(B)(1)(b)

Differs from Federal Rule by adding: (b) A party who has a privilege regarding part or all of the testimony of a deponent must either assert the privilege at the deposition or lose the privilege as to that testimony for purposes of the action. A party who claims a privilege at a deposition may not at the trial offer the testimony of

227

the deponent pertaining to the evidence objected to at the deposition.

MINNESOTA
RULE 26.02(1)

Mirrors Federal Rule 26(b)(1), Para. 1

MISSISSIPPI
SECTION 13–1–226(b)(1)

Mirrors Federal Rule 26(b)(1), Para. 1

MISSOURI
RULE 56.01(b)(1)

Mirrors Federal Rule 26(b)(1), Para. 1

MONTANA
RULE 26(b)(1)

Mirrors Federal Rule 26(b)(1), Para. 1

NEBRASKA
RULE 25–1267.02

Substantially similar to Federal Rule 26(b)(1), Para. 1. When referring to persons having knowledge, "relevant" substituted for "discoverable" facts.

NEVADA
RULE 26(b)(1)

Mirrors Federal Rule 26(b)(1), Para. 1

NEW HAMPSHIRE
RULE 35(b)(1)

Mirrors Federal Rule 26(b)(1), Para. 1

RULE 44, Para. 1

The deponent, on deposition or on written interrogatory, shall ordinarily be required to answer all questions not subject to privilege or excused by the statute relating to depositions, and it is not grounds for refusal to answer a particular question that the testimony would be inadmissible at the trial if the testimony sought appears reasonably calculated to lead to the discovery of admissible evidence and does not violate any privilege.

NEW JERSEY
RULE 4:10–2(a)

Substantially similar to Federal Rule 26(b)(1), Para. 1 except that subsection (a) has added "Nor is it ground for objection that the examining party has knowledge of the matters as to which discovery is sought."

NEW MEXICO
RULE 1–026(B)(1)

Mirrors Federal Rule 26(b)(1), Para. 1

NEW YORK
SECTION 3101(b)

Privileged Matter. Upon objection by a party privileged matter shall not be obtainable.

NORTH CAROLINA
RULE 26(b)(1)

Substantially similar to Federal Rule 26(b)(1), Para. 1 except that subsection (1) has added "Nor is it ground for objection that the examining party has knowledge of the information as to which discovery is sought."

NORTH DAKOTA
RULE 26(b)(1)

Mirrors Federal Rule 26(b)(1), Para. 1

OHIO
RULE 26(B)(1)

Mirrors Federal Rule 26(b)(1), Para. 1

OKLAHOMA
SECTION 3203(B)(1)

Mirrors Federal Rule 26(b)(1), Para. 1

OREGON
RULE 36(B)(1)

Substantially the same as Federal Rule 26(b)(1), Para. 1 except for some different language.

PENNSYLVANIA
RULE 4003.1

Substantially similar to Federal Rule 26(b)(1), Para. 1. Scope of discovery is subject to Rules 4003.2 to 4003.5 inclusive and Rule 4011.

RULE 4011(c)

Limitation of Scope of Discovery and Deposition. No discovery or deposition shall be permitted which relates to matter which is privileged.

RHODE ISLAND
RULE 26(b)(1)

Substantially similar to Federal Rule 26(b)(1), Para. 1. Scope of examination subject to Rule 30(b) or (d).

SOUTH CAROLINA
RULE 26(b)(1)

Mirrors Federal Rule 26(b)(1), Para. 1

SOUTH DAKOTA
SECTION 15–6–26(b)

Mirrors Federal Rule 26(b)(1), Para. 1

TENNESSEE
RULE 26.02(1)

Mirrors Federal Rule 26(b)(1), Para. 1

TEXAS
RULE 166b(3)(e)

Exemptions. The following matter(s) are not discoverable: (e) any matter protected from disclosure by privilege.

UTAH
RULE 26(b)(1)

Mirrors Federal Rule 26(b)(1), Para. 1

VERMONT
RULE 26(b)(1)

Mirrors Federal Rule 26(b)(1), Para. 1

VIRGINIA
RULE 4:1(b)(1)

Mirrors Federal Rule 26(b)(1), Para. 1

RULE 4:1(b)(5)

Limitations on Discovery in Certain Procedures. In any proceeding (1) for separate maintenance, divorce, or annulment of marriage, (2) for the exercise of the right of eminent domain, or (3) for a writ of habeas corpus or in the nature of coram nobis: (a) the scope of discovery shall extend only to matters which are relevant to the issues in the proceeding and which are not privileged.

WASHINGTON
RULE 26(b)(1)

Mirrors Federal Rule 26(b)(1), Para. 1

WEST VIRGINIA
RULE 26(b)(1)

Mirrors Federal Rule 26(b)(1), Para. 1

WISCONSIN
SECTION 804.01(2)(a)

Mirrors Federal Rule 26(b)(1), Para. 1

WYOMING
RULE 26(b)(1)

Mirrors Federal Rule 26(b)(1), Para. 1

†